Praise for *Jam*

'Robert Eisenman's *James the Brother of Jesus* is less a book than an irresistible force. Once opened . . . [it] bulldozes your prejudices, flattens your objections, elbows aside your counter-arguments, convinces you' — *Toronto Globe and Mail*

'Encyclopaedic . . . fascinating' — Karen Armstrong, *The Times*

'Powerful . . . expert . . . A thrilling essay in historical detection this passionate quest for the historical James refigures Christian origins' — *The Guardian*

'Eisenman is too careful a historian and too passionate a believer to attempt merely to debunk two thousand years of history. His is not an effort to replace Jesus with James, but to rescue the younger brother from the oblivion to which the blatantly fictionalized Book of Acts consigned him . . . Eisenman's course through the evidence is so logical and his narrative so compelling that one emerges after one thousand pages wondering how this demythologized, internally consistent understanding of early Christianity could have been kept out of sight for so long' — *The Scotsman*

'Blown away! The breadth and detail of Eisenman's investigations are breathtaking, as are its implications . . . Eisenman shows us how to crack the codes of theological disinformation, to listen to the long-faded echoes, to find handholds up what seemed an insurmountable climb to a peak from which to view the hitherto unseen landscape of early Christianity . . . Mind-blowing . . . Breathtaking . . . A Masterpiece!' — *The Journal of Higher Criticism*

'Fascinating reading' — *The Kirkus Review*

'What a book! Impressive in elegance and painstaking scholarship . . Magnificent ... A tour de force' — Neil Asher Silberman, author of *The Hidden Scrolls*

'A tremendous work of historical scholarship ... Expert ... Fascinating ... Unparalleled ... Apocalyptic ... A great book' — *The Jerusalem Post*

'Enthralling . . . immense . . . Compelling . . . Massive in its learning and relentless in its argument . . . *James the Brother of Jesus* offers a stunning reinterpretation of 'Jamesian Christianity' as the very opposite of the Christianity that has come down to us. Eisenman's book places us at the center of these controversies with often surprising results . . . It delivers us into an unfamiliar world of punning wordplay, trenchant allusion, and ruthless polemic, where nothing – including the person of Jesus – is quite what it seems . . . In helping us return to and deepening our understanding of Christianity's origins, Eisenman has done a service to believer and sceptic alike . . . A massive display of provocative scholarship' — *The Oregonian*

'Eisenman is like the Renaissance scientists, who had to hand-craft all the intricate parts of a planned invention. His book is an ocean of instructive insight and theory, a massive and profound achievement' — Robert M. Price, author of *Deconstructing Jesus*

'This book will live and live and live!' — A. Auswaks, Reviewer, *The Jerusalem Post*

'I permanently admire (this) superb book' — Harold Bloom, author of *Jesus and Yahweh: The Names Divine*

THE NEW JERUSALEM

A MILLENNIUM POETIC/PROPHETIC TRAVEL DIARIO,

1959-62

Robert Eisenman is the co-author of *The Facsimile Edition of the Dead Sea Scrolls* and *The Dead Sea Scrolls Uncovered* and the author of the bestselling *James the Brother of Jesus* and *The New Testament Code*. He is Professor of Middle East Religions and Archaeology and Director of the Institute for the Study of Judeo-Christian Origins at California State University Long Beach; and Visiting Senior Member of Linacre College, Oxford University.

He holds a B.A. from Cornell University, 1958 in Philosophy and Engineering Physics, an M.A. from N.Y.U, 1966 in Hebrew and Near Eastern Studies, and a Ph. D. from Columbia University, 1971 in Middle East Language and Cultures. He was a Senior Fellow at the Oxford Centre for Postgraduate Hebrew Studies and a United States National Endowment for the Humanities Fellow-in-Residence at the Albright Institute of Archaeological Research in Jerusalem where the Dead Sea Scrolls first came in and received their initial inspection.

In 1987-92, he was the leader of the worldwide campaign to break the academic and scholarly monopoly over the Dead Sea Scrolls, freeing them for research and, as a consequence, the consultant to the Huntington Library of San Marino, California on its decision to allow free access to its archives. In 2002-2003 he was the first to publicly announce that "the James Ossuary" was fraudulent, and he did so on the same day it appeared on the basis of the inscription itself and what it said, not as a result of any external 'scientific' or 'pseudo-scientific' measurements.

The poems in this travel collection do not represent any of these more scholarly endeavors. Rather, they are an actual transcript of the notes and jottings he kept between July, 1959 and August, 1962 when in a more youthful embodiment (but hopefully nonetheless creative), he was "on the road" some forty-five years ago between San Francisco and India with myriad stops in New York, Paris, Israel, Leicestershire, Cyprus, Turkey, Iran, Beleuchistan, and Pakistan. These thoughts do not represent his consciousness now, but rather his frame-of-mind then — when he was young.

By the same Author

The New Testament Code: The Cup of the Lord, the Damascus Covenant, and the Blood of Christ, Sterling/Barnes and Noble, 2006

James the Brother of Jesus, Penguin, 1998

The Dead Sea Scrolls and the First Christians, Harper Collins, 1996

The Dead Sea Scrolls Uncovered, Penguin, 1992

A Facsimile Edition of the Dead Sea Scrolls, Biblical Archaeology Society, 1991

James the Just in the Habakkuk Pesher, E. J. Brill, Leiden, 1986

Maccabees, Zadokites, Christians and Qumran: A New Hypothesis of Qumran Origins, E. J. Brill, Leiden, 1984

Islamic Law in Palestine and Israel, E. J. Brill, Leiden, 1976

THE NEW JERUSALEM

A MILLENNIUM POETIC/PROPHETIC TRAVEL DIARIO,1959-62

ROBERT EISENMAN

North Atlantic Books
Berkeley, California

Published by
North Atlantic Books
P.O. Box 12327
Berkeley, California 94712

Cover photo and original idea by Judith Turner
Back cover photo: The author as a young man sitting in front
of the Parthenon, January, 1959
Cover and book design by Susan Quasha
Printed in the United States of America

The New Jerusalem: A Millennium Poetic/Prophetic Travel Diario is sponsored by the Society for the Study of Native Arts and Sciences, a nonprofit educational corporation whose goals are to develop an educational and crosscultural perspective linking various scientific, social, and artistic fields; to nurture a holistic view of arts, sciences, humanities, and healing; and to publish and distribute literature on the relationship of mind, body, and nature.

North Atlantic Books' publications are available through most bookstores. For further information, call 800-337-2665 or visit our website at www.northatlanticbooks.com. Substantial discounts on bulk quantities are available to corporations, professional associations, and other organizations. For details and discount information, contact our special sales department.

Library of Congress Cataloging-in-Publication Data
Eisenman, Robert H.
The new Jerusalem : a millenium poetic/prophetic travel diario, 1959/1962 / by Robert Eisenman.
p. cm.
Summary: "Presents a poetic account in free verse of the author's travels as a young man through Europe, the Middle East, and Asia between 1959 and 1962"—Provided by publisher.
ISBN-13: 978-1-55643-637-6
ISBN-10: 1-55643-637-8
I. Title.
PS3605.I844N49 2007
811'.6—dc22

2006039125

1 2 3 4 5 6 7 8 9 SHERIDAN 14 13 12 11 10 09 08 07

Besides the streams of Babylon we sat and wept when we remembered Zion, leaving our harps hanging on the poplars there. For we had been asked to sing to our captors, to entertain those who had carried us off. "Sing," they said, "some Hymns of Zion." How could we sing a song of the Lord in a foreign country? Jerusalem, if I forget thee, may my right hand forget itself. May my tongue cleave to the roof of my mouth if I do not raise Jerusalem above the highest of my joys.

— Psalm 137:1-6

Shout for joy, you Heavens, exult you earth, Break forth you mountains into singing. For the Lord has comforted His people and has had compassion on His downcast ones. Zion has said, "The Lord has forsaken me, the Lord has forgotten me." Can a woman forget the baby at her breast or fail to cherish the son of her womb? Yet, even if these did (forget), I will not forget you. Behold I have engraven you upon the palms of My hands. Your walls are continually before Me. Your descendants draw near while your despoilers and destroyers depart.

— Isaiah 49:7-13

TABLE OF CONTENTS

INTRODUCTION

The poems in this collection were written from1959–62 just as they appear. They have not been altered or improved. They represent, at once, a travel *diario* in free verse and a *bildungsroman* depicting a young man's passage from boyhood to manhood. They also represent a spiritual journey or quest and, in parts, are even what some might call "prophetic." The reader will have to judge this for him or herself.

The young man (obviously myself) leaves San Francisco in the summer of 1959 at the height of the "Beatnik" episode there, after having thrown his cards away while on line in the Registration Hall at UC Berkeley to do graduate work in Comparative Literature, hitch-hikes across America to New York, and, from thence, on to Paris — at that time the center of the artistic or spiritual universe then referred to as "the Bohemian world." Once in Paris, he faces certain challenges, mostly social and physical, but also intellectual and sexual; and then sets off for the East down through Yugoslavia, Greece, and Turkey (the fabled 'Orient Express,' though not so fabulous then) and on to Israel — most notably working at kibbutzim in the hills of Northern Galilee, but also meeting his unbeknown-previously-to-him family.

From there, he returns to Paris and New York, pursuing a lost love just in time to work on the Kennedy Election Campaign, the nomination of whom he had greeted with hopeful enthusiasm as he disembarked from a Turkish Haifa-to-Marseille passenger ship in Piraeus, Greece in July, 1960. Disillusioned in both (as well as what followed), he returns to Europe — first back to Paris and then to teach in the winter of 1961 in the English Leicestershire countryside. With the coming of spring, he sets off once more on his journey to and quest for spiritual enlightenment represented in those days by the idea of "India," only to again get sidetracked — this time in Teheran after having, once more, crossed through Turkey and Iran — by an offer to join the new Peace Corps.

He returns in one day via the miracle of jet travel, all the way back to where he began in Berkeley, California — in the period before the student protests began there — to be a part of the first group about to be sent into the field (the long exhortation, "*America, I Call upon You,*" in Part Two, *On to Provence*, becoming something of an anthem for that group). But while it went on to meet President Kennedy on the White House lawn and to Africa and Ghana, he rather returned directly to New York and Paris to pursue his original quest in all seriousness. India was his goal, not Ghana and Africa, and he was going to go on to India whatever the cost and whatever the hardship — either physically or spiritually. This was his charge to himself.

Once more he returns to Israel with renewed determination ("the Land of his Ancestors/"the Land of his Forefathers," as he terms it in the poems) to work on kibbutzim and, after much soul-searching — including stays at various monasteries around the country and encountering the nascent 'Judeo-Christian Community' there and a fight in Tel Aviv with the owner of the socially and artistically '*chic*' California Cafe (the future Israeli "Peace Pilot" and "Peace Ship" patron-to-be, Abie Nathan) — he undergoes what appears to be a real spiritual enlightenment. This and the insights in Part Four, "*The Cup of Trembling*," constitute the first climax of the book. There will be a second.

This time he does set forth in the spring of his twenty-fifth year to India, completing his "*Passage to India*" and the spiritual journey it represented in the summer of 1962 in India while sleeping outside on a rope bed in the courtyard of the Jewish Synagogue in New Delhi approximately two and a half months before the Cuban Missile Crisis; and the final 'Enlightenment' is for the reader to discover. To complete the celebratory/'prophetic' aspect of this work, the author has added an "Afterword": "Words Written after the U.N. Security Council Debate, 5/19/67" and "Six-Day War Triumph Poems."

The book is also meant to be read as an answer to those who thought all intellectual and artistic endeavor in the late Fifties and early Sixties began and ended with "the Beats" and for those who did not agree with the ideological orientation of their approach or of that "Generation" — a movement the author considers to have contributed much to the intellectual malaise and artistic decline of the country. In that sense, it might be considered an '*anti-Beat Manifesto*' — written in the same period but from an opposite perspective.

It is also meant to be read for whatever uplift and spiritual and religious insight and exhilaration it might provide. In particular, those who are either monotheistically-inspired or immersed in or enamored of the Bible and its prophetical approach may find something that will be congenial or moving in it.

Whatever personal comments — positive or negative — that are made through the course of the quest-journey are meant to confront reality and contribute to the reader's own confrontation with reality, not to either hurt it or be purposefully insulting or injurious. Rather, they are meant to conserve authenticity and provide a genuine picture of the metamorphosis of a young man's psychological and religious consciousness without editorialization and without revision. In like manner, the reader should realize that the voice in the free verse/poetry or prophecy is not that of the writer today but his of some forty or more years ago — "forty years in the wilderness" as it were. "Forty years" perhaps were what was necessary for the point-of-view, presented here as faithfully and honestly as possible, to be appreciated.

It is to be hoped, as well, that the reader from whatever denomination or political/religious orientation will be able to participate in the biblically-inspired and sometimes even intoxicated mindset herein expressed, taking it in the spirit in which it was intended — that of fellowship and communion and not of confrontation. Then, too, it is hoped that the individual reader will be able to free him or herself from whatever shackles might have previously bound them or from whatever preconceptions they might have been subject to, or whatever authority.

The style, as stated, is sometimes poetic and sometimes prophetic, a style it is felt that has particular relevance for the presentday lack of new and vital religio-poetic expression. In Deuteronomy 18:14-22, when speaking of "the True Prophet," the believer or adept is cautioned not to pre-judge the individual in question but rather to listen to and see which of his words come to pass. In the case of *The New Jerusalem*, it is hoped the reader will take this admonition to heart and in the end judge for him or herself which have or whether they have.

Robert Eisenman
Fountain Valley, California
February, 2007

PROLOGUE

July, 1959- February, 1960

July 28th, 1959:

Crossing Oakland Bay Bridge
and looking back at the City
of San Francisco disappearing:

A new year beginneth.

And so it has come to
an end
And there is nothing
But me at its end.
But it is starting again —
Another and, then,
Another after that.
I leave a city I love,
But I must — I must.
I am a man and I must
Live the way I must.

They have taught you much,
But mostly to stand tall
And be sure of the destiny
you must create.
You go to face many debili-
tating moments
And you must be well-armed.
I am telling you this, so you
May read it again and *know*.

And see the city — see the city,
The sun sinking behind it in the West,
The shadows of its buildings
Lengthening in the reddish light —
A deep heaviness, your soul.

I will not tell you how it is but
You must remember — remember!
Keep the excitement in your life,
No pressures, no people sneering
"loafer" at you.
You must settle and work in calm.
One day, return — and now on to
Europe (sickness, conscious one).

A boy standing out all day
in the middle of Nevada
in the sun hitchhiking:

The will to
Go on is
Only human.

A book to sell —
Entitle it '*America,*' because
They want to know how shitty they are.

Boy and girl,
And night
Together.

Somewhere in the Morning in Utah

July 1th, 1959

On what the man who gave you
a ride last night to Salt Lake City
said:

They are not happy — the machines,
The sterile comforts, the unnecessary
products,
Their youth divided against itself.
One time they had great hope —
Now no more — now there will be
Only bitterness and much suffering.
Because this generation *knows*,
This people is sick — perhaps.

Autumn Leaves

October 14th, 1959 —
On a street in Paris:

And nine months
Is but a day.
And so you thought
I had gone away,
So you thought it
Could end that way
And all that passed
Is but the same?

Long, long have I waited,
Long, long for thee.
Hear his steps —
The hunter's tread
Moves towards the lair.

Hear, O fates, and mock
me not,
For I shall wait freezing
on this street
Till night does spread
Its soft October blanket
Over the darkening twilight
of this city's chill.

Mock me not, my friends
For I am he who travels with the night —
Mock not he who travels with the night.

Poems for a Love

Yes and I feel that I am on thin ice —
Ice floes floating on the swift current.
And each step, each step is precarious,
each one unsure,
Touching carefully, then forward —
Plunging on, not recklessly, but certainly.
And others — falling away down the
stream,
Pulled by the rushing water away.
Yes and I am almost there, almost to
the other side.
I see it there in all its whiteness —
white so white,
And I step on, for I am almost across.

Love

It is like a tug-of-war —
Both sides pulling
And then one side,
Slowly, relentlessly,
Carrying the other —
Not over-confident,
Allowing for reversal,
Not certain until the
last man
Is dragged across the line
And then the jubilant
shouts,
The cries of victory.

And it will happen now, it will happen now.
All the signs have pointed to it, all the omens.
Every bit of what happened was for this,
And it will be something completely new,
starting out together anew.
All the dreams have foretold it, all the portents —
And all the others will be meaningless and
there will be only this.
Both of us starting out together anew —
A new adventure, a new life, a new world.

This is so right
And she knows it too,
For we are man and woman,
Together we are man and woman —
And she will come to me tonight
And she will know it tonight,
For all the rest fall away
And there is only this.

But be careful, love,
I warn you, be careful —
I am not as the others.
You should know that now.
I am different — I am
well-armed.
When you come near me,
There is no going away.

There is secret talk between lovers,
Waves that travel beneath the sea,
So that what appears one way to others
Is very different for two lovers.

It grows like all things imperceptibly,
Like a tooth or a young boy,
A breast in puberty —
A bud to a leaf, a seed to a tree.
And then one day it bursts forth
With no hint of how or from where
it came.

How often do I worry
That, when I see you,
We shall touch some note
And only bitterness
Will come forth. But, oh,
How pointless such a worry,
For there is so much
Love for you in me
That reproaches are
But flakes of snow
Upon a boundless sea.

Can it be that
When you say no,
I know it is yes?
Can such unreason be?

Am I above them all
Destined to be happy?

Ah love,
If we could but realize
These things together —
That all the rest
Are as the weather
And this alone endures?

Ah love,
Make your life with me,
For together we shall know
Such lovely days.

Ah love,
Make your life with me,
For separate there shall only
Be those empty days.

Now it is my tide,
My time has come,
And I too,
Rising with the flood.

Run, quarry, run!
For the hunter
Now has come.

Now we shall see
Their images too *forgotten*
As I was long *forgotten*.

These moments were
So easily *forgotten*,
Because they were
Never more *begotten*.

Love's Fear

Yes, and there was something in her voice,
The way she threw it up to me so blatantly —
All the others she had known, all the others,
For I knew there had been others,
That she had been with others —
I could hear it in her voice.
It was nothing rational,
Nothing intellectual, you see,
Just something I sensed, something I knew.
And there was something else too,
Something I had known all along,
All those nights at the beginning alone
Thinking of her with other men —
That the most terrifying image of all.
And why I asked myself, why not
After they too had gone?
But I know now. I could hear it in her voice —
The fear now that I had come back.

Could I, love,
Be some ogre?
Could I,
Who could
Not hurt you,
Scare you so?

Cruel love, how many times have you smote me —
How many times have you brought me low?
"From where are you getting your money?"
you asked.
And I suppose I can tell you — why not tell you?
There's no sense hiding it — and my letters,
Had you thought of destroying them too?

O cruel love,
You revel in telling me,
"We left the game at halftime."

And I loved you,
And what did you do?
Throw it all away.

And I loved you —
You can bet I loved you,
And what did you do?
Throw it all away.

And I loved you,
And what did you do,
Knowing I loved you?
Throw yourself to all
the rest.

And it is past, but what is it I have
left behind,
What is it I have given you and you
have given me —
Some charm, some elixir, so life
transformed can live?
For all those others possess it not.
Yes I, too, have known others,
Many others — seen their faces,
Wandered from one to one,
Seeking what? A woman's form,
her shoulder,
The skin drawn smooth attracting,
The flesh so soft — a thigh, a leg?
But no, it dwells not there, the chase,
the hunt,
One night and then it is done.
My hollow, hollow eyes, looking down
and never up,
Those hollow stares, the eyes so lost —
No light, no flash of joy, the life far gone.
And what is it I have lost to you and is it
now lost?
Have you not also lost that thing to me?
And why was it so necessary,
Why for you and why for me?
And has it made us strong,
Am I now man and you now woman?
I suppose it has and yet I wonder,
If ever we two do meet again, is that
thing too now past?

How many times have
I called your name
And how many times
Have you not answered
it?

February 6th, 1960

And there is so much love in you,
So much loved stored up in everyone —
And when you think
You cannot smile anymore,
When you think
It has all dried up
Or you have all run dry,
You are wrong
And it is only the barriers
Set up between peoples that speak —
Only the fear, the pride,
And it only takes but one soft touch
To let it all pour forth again.

We are free upon the land.

I am myself
And by these words
A little boy again.

Trust nothing of
What is written,
For another man
Will come along
And write it again.
Trust only the man
And the spirit you
feel
As it carries you
along.

PART ONE

THE COMING TO THE EAST

1960

Turkey

And man shall have dominion,
Man shall have dominion over
His flocks,
The birds of the air — the fish of
the sea.

The coming of spring —
Thin mist, leaves,
Pools of muddy water
Sparkling beside the tracks.

The shepherds alone
And the flocks,
The animals clustered
Around, following.

Great white and black birds
Like pelicans — Louisiana.

Great white and black birds with red legs,
Perched upon the rooftops,
Amid the people and the villages —
Standing on the trees.

The land uncultivated,
The land lying to waste.
Only a strip here, a strip
there
To suffice for feeding.

And lo, the water,
Lo, a more
Industrious people — the French.

French knights riding to and fro.
— Villehardouin's *Chronicle of the Crusades*

Shepherd's Song

And every day the train came
And every day I lifted my arms
and waved.

His not to understand
The rhythms of his life —
His but to adhere and adjust.

The people clustered
About the railroad stations
Waiting for the event.

The children coming
Running, happy smiles,
The children playing —
Hair cropped short,
All looking the same.
The children better than
their elders,
More at ease in the
world.

O know what it is to be an adult,
See the faces lean and dangerous.

No wonder there are wars,
No wonder men fight,
No wonder politics,
Governments, and crusades.

See the women
Grown like stumps.

The Coming into Israel

O Israel, where hast thou scattered
my People,
O Israel, where were they thrown,
From where have they gathered,
From where have they come?

And so I have come —
How long shall I stay,
How long must I stay,
What strange force is
    driving me on?

Kibbutz Sasa

And they have built
Their homes upon the
        rubble.
O how vain, what folly.
They live from day to day
        unseeing —
They have no defense
And yet they go on here
As if in another place.
At night a man can come
Into their camp to kill —
The wilderness sets them in
Yet their babies cry,
Their children shout.
They go on here not
Knowing as the ones before —
They shall not remain and
Their ruins too shall
        remain.
O Lord, is this folly
Not simply for fools?

And these too shall pass,
Built upon the rubble of
Those that came before.

A part of
My life I owe.
But not the whole.

I have left a part of
me with you,
my love.

My world resides where
You reside, my love,
And every day is
But an adventure
Until I return to you.

It is a joy to
Hear your voice,
A delight, a sorrow.
I charge thee,
Do not give thyself
To any other
Until I see you
once again.

If only spirits
Could walk abroad
When summoned up.
I would call
Her spirit to me,
Bid it walk across
The earth and enter
mine.
Why cannot spirits
In this way entwine?

Another thing has come —
Not that thing.
I am not so weak as that.

I came to Israel
Because God was
To make me strong
And now I must stay.

On the Northern Road

And now I shall overcome all my
fears —
Fear of men, fear of death,
Fear of the land, fear of fish,
Fear of snakes, fear in the fields,
Fear at night, fear of fighting,
Fear of knives, fear of killing,
fear of working.
I shall work where the men work,
Rise when they rise, sleep where
they sleep —
In the fields, in the sea, eat what
they eat,
Live what they live, be what they
are;
For I am called — called to the Land
Of other men before me, their spirits,
To finish what was then begun.
Hear O Israel, I have come.

And all these things are like a
tent stake,
Setting down the line and making
it taut,
No action more beyond that line,
beyond that point.
A law is set, having lived lived
on —
No more holding, no more crying,
Go with it, let it go, leave it, make
it mine.

The simplest of rhythms —
A rhythm like within
My heart.

A night of moon
And lightened sky.

To know what other men's spirits
As sensitive as my own
Have grasped.

Ah great Shakespeare,
You needed not
Experience as your teacher
And yet thou knew
As much or more than I.

The human behaviour
Is like a book
With each new day, a page;
Each new mood, a chapter —
A fear, an exultation.

The joy
Of creation
Is in the original.

There were our fathers
And there are us.
Let each man say,
"This is my time
And I am glad."

I did a small thing,
But the thing was small
When it was done.

For her
I write
These lines.

Let
Each day
Be grand.

And the Lord said:
"*Put off thy glasses,
For thou needest not
To see things far off.
Thou shalt see things
Close up and at hand.*"

And they shall come upon thee
And ask, "How do we know thee?"
And thou shalt answer,
"I *am he that is sent by the Lord."*
And they shall look upon thee strangely
But thou shall not turn away.

Thou shall fear no fear,
No thing,
For the Lord walkest with thou.

The Lord has commanded,
"*Go down to the waters and, yea, fish.*"
And thou shalt go down to the waters
and, yea, fish.

The Lord said,
"*Take thee up from this land,*
Take thee up from thy father's house,
From thy father's keep, and get thee gone"
And He shall multiply thee
As thy father Isaac and thy father Jacob,
Make thy seed fertile and increase thee.

And thou shall walkest
as one blind.
Thou shall see no thing
Before thee or afar off,
And in this way
Will He test thy metal,
For thou walkest
As the man by the day
With no knowledge or
Fear of the morrow,
Greeting each new thing
As it comes, as He sends
it.

And thou shall inherit
The gift of thy fathers,
Walk as the prophet Moses
With the sight of the Lord,
For He has made Himself known
unto thee —
He is in thy heart.

And men shall ask,
"Who is this man?"
And they shall know thee
As they once knew thee,
As thy father's son —
One who was young and loved;
And they shall love thee
for that.
But they shall not know
thee
As thou really art.

And, if thou speakest with
The tongue of foreigners,
It is meet for, lo,
Thou speakest unto foreigners.

And thou shalt dwell
Forty days in the wilderness
And then return among them.

Lo,
An East wind
Has come unto thee.

Ah love, how I waited for thy
answer —
How I waited, how I waited,
But it did not come and now
it's done.

And now I'm free —
To where, to what,
Being free?
And is it true,
I had already
Outgrown you?

My heart is ripe
And opens unto thee
As a flower to the tree.
But thou art gone,
No more to open unto me.

Ah love,
I do not
Know thee
Anymore.

Sleep comes
This night
But slowly.
Be still,
My voices,
I bid thee.

On the Path at Night

O bird outside my window,
What noises dost thou make?

I go out
In the night
On pointed toes
To drink of water.

O bird in the tree,
How I long for thee.

Come bite me serpent,
If that be my fate —
Better now than late.

I know the phases
And the fates —
The heavens and
the tides.

The spigot throws,
The water flows.

July will be my making —
June too soon, August too late.
How do we know these things?
They are simply fate.

It is like
Cleaning out
The hollow mind
And starting fresh.

From what spring,
In what earth,
To what music,
Shall I drink,
May I plant,
Will I sing?

Keep your motives pure.
Follow not the stag, the hunt,
Follow not the adventurer's cunt,
But go thou where the odour's pure.

What is in me is
Like milk in a cow's udder.
Sometimes it is fertile
And I may draw —
And sometimes it runs dry
And I must be careful
Not to overdraw,
Lest I damage that
Which is so delicate.

Draw, but
Do not overdraw.
Drink, but be not greedy.

I hear a lonely piano in the night
And my mind drifts back across the waste
To her — that one, a time ago.

The clouds pass silently the moon,
white and halved.
Before the night was white and the
moon was whole.

I try to think of thoughts then thought,
But the sounds of now break the mirror.
I try to feel that languor once felt,
But only a deep sadness rises in its stead.

Ah her, could it be, to be past?
Ah her, what strange dreams, what soft
odours —
And will that odour still remain?
Ah her, where more in time or space
Come orange blossoms on the breeze?

The path leads the way I go,
Through frankincense
To India.

O Lord, I cannot fight against the
flood,
I cannot live mediocrely.
So, whatever my mistakes may be,
Forgive them, Thou to me.

If thou were
A thousand miles,
I would come.
But thou are
No longer thee,
And I no longer
me.

The way's the way
And none's to say
Thou should have
gone
A different one.

Evermore, evermore,
And I shall love
Thee
Evermore.

I go to a place
Because it goes
with me.

My ancestors,
I am with thee
In thy fate.

Journey to Jerusalem
— "A day of dappled, seaborne clouds"
Joyce

Have you ever frolicked with the
sea —
Black flag up on an empty beach,
Breakers rolling in
One white upon the next?
No sea, not this time, I'm not for
thee.

A great sadness weights upon my
soul
Of people, lost places, and things.

On the Road to Jerusalem

To come late at night to an empty home,
To come in the night on the road to Jerusalem,
Up the hills and trees from the plain —
The road winding a way wound so many ages before,
The moon white and splendid on the hollow hills.

Sabbath Eve on the Streets of Jerusalem

Do you know, I think I would go ten
thousand miles
If I thought it would draw from her
Those soft and lovely tears just once?

It has been told me often
By others very close,
She does not love me —
I too would think like this.

I am glad too
That I am going,
For now it is
That I am free.

Tonight the moon
Is full and it
Goes with me.

An intolerable sadness is upon me,
Of nights, of lofty breezes,
Of soft odours.

I want to go and see
My cousin tonight —
O pray that she is in.

No, I will
Not lie
With her
Tonight —
No, no, no...

Some ineffable sweetness is upon me.
I will rip my clothes from off my back,
I will go naked and exposed,
I will cross a thousand lands —
Sleep in a thousand streets.
I shall be one of them,
Immersed in them, and they all part of me.

Cry O cry,
Die away,
Ye gentle hearts.

If thou were me and I were thee,
Then thou wouldst feel
This sadness instead of me.
O how wonderful that would be,
If thou were me and I were thee.

With such strangeness,
Go back and claim her.

Go back,
Go back.

GO BACK!
GO BACK!

There was the moon full now
With Venus and two trees,
And I had been right —
It had been trying to tell me
something.

All in harmony,
The touch and touch
Of small and big.

Passage to India

The elastic band is stretched,
Two beings pulling apart, then broken —
The distance now between them running,
too great.

And now that one end is broken,
The other seems to fall away
And nothing's left of
All that storm save me, emerging.

There was a dense forest
And suddenly
The trees fell down.

PART TWO

ON TO PROVENCE

1960–61

The Mediterranean facing Venus

Back to man
To live
With man.

The Mediterranean facing
South:

Patterns of the stars,
Tracings on dark nights.

And men roamed the seas
From Phoenicia and Canaan
To Greece and Rome —
And the warm seas brought
forth life.

The Goddess Athena
Put these words
In her mouth.

To the Candidate Kennedy, July 17th, 1960

(On getting off the ship at Piraeus and reading *The Herald Tribune*)

A new force is rising
Out of America, a new star.
A man is born who speaks my
words.
From out the waste and chaos
of defeat,
A new hope and a new light —
My heart goes with him.

On the Acropolis

To an Israeli girl:

And we have
Our goddesses too.

Ah Aphrodite, if you
Could still but see,
How jealous you
Would have been,
For up your very steps,
On your very rock,
In your very shrine,
Stood another this day
As lovely as thee.

The Aeolian Isles:

Stromboli — a cone-shaped volcano,
The two lights of its jetty
In the shadowy haze.

On to Provence

I do not plan or think ahead,
But take each moment as it comes —
The general arc, a thing of vision;
The everyday, a challenge to follow.

A poem that's redone is like
A day that's undone and,
Therefore, not poetry.

I have written out a code this night —
I will not take a job for my own gain.
And this I will consider as a creed,
I will serve, but not a man — some
Higher Thing.

There's the path — I see it right.
But when the path has not yet come,
A man should not hesitate or try his sight,
But wait and, waiting, it will come.

This is the path to follow —
My whole body says it,
My heart and spirit say it too.

Paris

A new man shall walk this earth,
Not a poet or philosopher,
Not a statesman or a conqueror —
But a new man, a man no man has
heretofore yet seen.

America, I Call upon You

And if thy time has ever come, it has come now, it is on thee now,
And if thou are to live or die, the time is now, the choice is thine.
Oh yes, thou shall endure, as others have endured — all things, in
fact, endure —
It is not this, I thee adjure, for even rocks, they too endure.
But if it be thy spirit which shall flourish and go on, if it be
this — now failing,
Yes, flare up once more, light a way — that time is now.

For an old era now falls away. Unseen it slips so silently. No,
others cannot see that it is done.
Fifteen years have passed since the last Great War, but I tell thee
it is dying now, now fading out,

That which began a hundred years before, that which grew from a land once brave and strong,
That which flickered and went out in the swarms of men — that hope turned sour, that honour lost,
Attracting not the souls of men as at thy birth but bringing forth their lust instead —
America the land of plenty, the land of promise, America the land of greed.
That which could have lived if only Lincoln lived — that which found its loftiest expression
Before a flood of spoil, a flood of greed, a flood of mediocrity blotted if from your soul.

And had that great man lived, had that bullet not have found its mark,
Would all that then was good and strong not have died? Perhaps.
But others came, others trampling on your heart — small men, blind men,
A new era, a general not made to suffer thus the souls of men —
And all that once was bright within you withered and went out,
All that idealism of thy fathers, all of Jefferson, Franklin, and of Paine —
All that went out and a new man appeared, a man grown of seeds sown by Jackson,
But without his honour, without his pride — all that too had died,
The very flower of which cut off in that Great War, cut off because it had to die,
Swarmed over by the Northern horde — fought bravely it is true,
But still foredoomed to die, fighting for a foredoomed cause.

All that went out, all that which was sweet and noble, all that which was gentle,

All that love of home, love of father, mother, sister, brother — all that went out
Because of one tragic shot and, America, you became lost and the flame within you died.
The Seventies came and the ants crawled in, your politics grew foul;
The Eighties and your population swelled — men in search of land and riches,
Few men in search of thee — the Nineties, and a new frivolity appeared,
A great, new class without a soul — men to run your new machines, men to run your businesses.
A few of you went back abroad, Henry James and Stephen Crane, Gertrude Stein,
Seeking something you had lost.

Then came the First Great War and you were puzzled; your youth was startled,
Saw a chance to reclaim honour, saw some glory — a shadow of that gone before.
You had the Escadrille and Ambulance Corps, men like John Dos Passos, E. E. Cummings, and William Faulkner;
And then ye followed, plunging blindly in at the end to swing the balance.
Your Wilson started out to set things right, but you could not understand and went back home —
Look at that poor meaninglessness, soldiers returning from the front,
No reason for why they had gone, no reason for why they returned.
The Twenties came, something had come and then been lost —
Men like Hemingway and Fitzgerald drank and amused themselves —
A flicker of carelessness before the end; your gangsters rose from out that swill.

Then came the crash, O how ye crashed — your younger souls embracing a foreign creed.
The others of you, long before been put to sleep, now turned their backs
While a monster grew, a monster sure enough — out of all the grimness of that poor struggle,
Out of all that supposedly had died, it reared its head,
While your courage failed, your memories fled, your hearts grew faint.

A million souls it turned to soap, ten million others blown away, ten million others long since dead,
And you watched while it devoured all that you had helped lay down,
Watched while only one brave land stood strong and bore its shock,
Thy mother land, the land thou fought two hundred years ago.
A few of you went, it is true, a few partook of those few hours,
But the most of you waited, long since lost, the trail now gone,
Covered over with the soot, covered over with the cars, covered over with the thousand signs.

And then they stung you, then you came, then you poured ten million men across the sea.
Then you woke and it matters not the reason for your sleep.
You crossed the globe from East to West, scattering your blood in every land —
And though you came so late, though you came of anger and not of pride,
Your honour was restored to you and the whole world held out its heart to you.
Your men were greeted in a hundred lands with naught save tears and cheers.

Frenchman and Jew lifted up their hands — yellow men, black
men, Muslim men,
Men from a thousand different lands, a thousand different fields,
A thousand different wombs — all men, even the vanquished paid
thee homage,
And so they offered up their trust, offered up their faith, that you
should bring about a lasting peace.

And you endeavored, it is true. You set upon the earth a Council
of Nations,
You opened up your heart and spread out your wealth for all the
world — enemy and friend alike;
But though your armies lingered on abroad, your soul had gone
back home,
And another struggle grew from out the last, a struggle you could
not see,
A struggle you did not understand, a struggle you did not wish to
understand;
And so you fought another war, a war more painful than any
other, a war that bled you,
A war with no apparent honour, a war you did not win, a war
where your men ran like frightened boys —
A bitter war where everything you stood for seemed to fail,
everything you believed in just a slogan
When what was real was dying, breaking in those prison camps,
cracking beneath the strain.

And you invented names, invented capitalism, invented idealism;
And you brought another general in to stem the tide, a man you
loved — a man less suited even than the other.
And so you staggered, so you withered and grew complacent, so
you sickened, so you fell.

He sent your emissaries around the world — businessmen, well-
meaning men, ignorant men —
These descendants of your robber barons, these descendants of
your carpet-baggers,
Not men of Monroe's, Madison's, or of Adams' day,
Not men of Whitman, Thoreau, or Emerson's kind — not even
men like Lee or Jackson,
But ignorant men, tiny men, blond-haired or blue-eyed men,
advertising men, soulless men;
Brutal men, parasitic men, redounding to your injury wherever
they are stationed;
And all the world watched you through these men, watched too
your tourists with their dollars,
And that gratitude, once so warm, was turned to scorn.

And why was that peace, so long sought, so dearly bought, so long
in coming?
And what was it you could not see, what was it that had gone
wrong,
What was it that should have ended — Europe with its hundred
nations,
That flame of fire ignited now within the East, those sounds of
battle
Carried down across the desert, reverberating now within the
jungles?

For believe me you are sick, believe me you are tottering.
Your forces stretch from East to West in all the world, fortifying
nothing, stemming nothing.
Abroad, your leader's name a thing of ridicule, your own a thing of
scorn;
While at home, your youth's astray — no thought of honour, no

thought of homage,
Pulled asunder by two worlds, Madison Avenue and the garbage
pail.
Television pumps its purposelessness into your millions: hoodlums,
gangsters, every man his car —
Motels road signs, hamburger stands; your best intentions
misinterpreted
Or distorted into propaganda — your worst revealed for all to
see;
Esso tankers looting the world, not flying your flag or giving your
name, but flying their own,
Time and *Life* the spokesmen for your soul; your world now
tottering, your soul now sick —
Your bombs, your rockets, your jingoistic capitalism, one man's
words like those of another's,
Your national service laughed at, avoided by your own — your
army served begrudgingly,
The best of your blood now fleeing away unwilling to serve —
the worst interested only in themselves,
While your lawyers grow richer, your doctors fatter.

But America, I tell thee that time's now done, that time's now
gone, that time is past, those men are done.
Fifteen years have passed since the last Great War. DeGaulle now
sits upon the throne of France.
The men and generals made in that poor time have made their
ascent, their time is gone.
A new race of men is now appearing — heraldic, I proclaim it, a
new era.
What has passed is past, no more to come — no longer Europe
or America,
No longer every man his own backyard, but now all the world.

Five hundred years it was in coming, five hundred years we suf-
suffered so,
And only now we see it dawning: no more the man in search of
spoil, no more the man in search of plunder,
But a new man — once more the giving, once more the honour,
once more the men of Lincoln's blood;
For no more can petty men, men lean of spirit, uphold your ho-
nour,
No more the bargainers, no more the public spoilers, ye the new
land, you the hope of man,
You the liberated ones. Your patriots now are coming —
That which was nurtured deep within your soul, you still the
guardian of that soul,
Men like Patrick Henry and Nathan Hale, men who'll fight not
just for you, but all the world,
To live and die for all the world, to give to all the world;
So every man may live, not simply eat, so all of men can hold up
their heads,
Not sell themselves for food or a ploughshare, but breathe freely,
breathe easily.

For if you are to live or die the time is now, the choice is thine;
If thou art to raise yourself, pull yourself once mighty from out
your slumber, the choice is thine;
For the whole world awaits you — the whole of man abides thy
coming
And, if ye are to stumble, ye stumble now. And this is the task I do
proclaim thee,
This is the task to which thou'art called; for you shall either forget
your self-enriching ways
And lift up your spirit or fall away, die out — no more the child
excused.

Walt Whitman, we have come —
Many poets, a land of them,
To harken to thy call.

With reverence for you,
In honour of you,
We accept the challenge,
Accept the bequest,

For truly, thou wert right.
Not in your own time was
Your honour to be wrought
But it is for us to justify you.

Walt Whitman, we have come,
Many poets, a land of them —
To do men honour, to sing
The soul of man again.

America, O hear my voice —
Bob Eisenman is but my name.
A Jew by birth, now one of you,
I come of an ancient race —
A line of prophets,
Now reborn to chant for thee.
America, be drawn by me.
Born of you, be charmed by me.

New York

Washington Square Village

Sitting alone among the rose trees,
The sound of sirens and the hums,
The empty buildings —
And the breeze of the Lord.

I am the poet of the milk machine.
I am the poet of our age.
I am the poet of reusable appliances
Of paper plates and straws.
I am the poet of disposability
And planned obsolescence —
I am the poet of our time.

My soul stoops down
On bended knees
To serve.

October 19th, 1960:

Tonight are all the ships
gone out to sea.
I think it's time to part.

Gird round thy waist My sword,
My son,
And, at My command, go forth.

Lines scrawled
upon a bridge
in Brooklyn:

To a dying love.

Behold thou art fair,
My beloved,
Fair, fair fair...

Reach
Your arms
About my back.

A Reaching Around of Arms
— Election Night, 1960 —

I hear America singing.
From out the waste,
The chaos of defeat,
The sounds come home.
From North and South
And East and West,
I hear the voices wakening.

November 8th,
1960:

The slate is
Wiped clean,
A new me —
A country
I can love.

November 9th, 1960:

A turning point has
Been reached. By just
The slightest bit
The ship has swung
Around in the breeze.
Move over a little,
Stop your ridiculing,
There is wind once
More in our sails.

President Kennedy

President Kennedy, I salute you, sir.
With you there ushers in the new era,
With you there comes the flowering age.
Perhaps you will not live to see it done,
Perhaps not even its fruition — who knows?
But you have ridden on the tide.
And though the balance was uncertain,
Though its conception was precarious,
The thing is done — a direction is set,
not now to be undone.

And what do men die for?
That a thing might grow,
That a thing might live and flower.
And what is a flower —
Though they may not have known it
then —
That thing which is flowering now.

Homer and Whitman

Homer, he was a blind poet who could see,
　　　　the precursor of an age,
And all these things are but the same.
It takes a million men, their vision set
　　　　and planted on the same,
No thing in isolation, no man apart,
But all working together, voyaging
　　　　towards that point:
A Pericles, a Thucydides, a Xenophon,
　　　　a Socrates —
All for the greater glory of that single thing,
For man and of man, for people and by
　　　　people, for all of man.

And no one is born apart,
No being dying not contributing,
No act of Brown or Lincoln,
No soldier fallen; no unsuccess, unsuccessful;
No man who wasted gone to waste,
No poet drunken, no junkie sunken,
No man of wisdom whose voice unheard,
No Smith or Wilkie, no thing that grew,
No act that was, no strand uncaught,
No thread unknitted in the final fabric.

And though it be in our time and
　　　　not another,
Though the final flowering finds
Some earth for its fruition,
Baked by our suns and others' suns,
Baked by our fathers' suns before us,
Though the blossom blossoms, blooming
　　　　in the summertime;
And though there is only one summer

for one flowering;
There was a springtime too, and a
wintertime before that.

And we have had our winter and our
springtimes.
Our patriots died and bled.
We have had our Homer, the precursor of
our age,
And though he came a hundred years ago,
Though he came at a time of trouble and
of strife,
He had his heroes to be sung,
Our heroes now, unreal men — grand images.

And others shall arise
And that voice shall still be heard.
A Kennedy shall arise from out the East,
A Johnson from out the South,
And others shall come from North and West,
To knit the wound that then was struck.
And we shall hear that voice sounded so
long ago,
Celebrate that act and dream, as he celebrated
it then,
Celebrate that celebration;
For America, truly, thy time has come.

And I shall be
The chronicler
Of that age.

That spirit which came down to me
From my father before me and his fathers,
That spirit which grew undamaged —
Though battered, battered by my mother's race,
A clan of monetary men though well-meaning —
Of fear and inhibition, that spirit of slavery,
That short success so pitifully enchained,
That spirit of the wandering Jew —
The wanderer, my great grandfather voyaging
to Jerusalem;
My grandmother whom I never saw — of warmth
and love and excellence.
My grandfather (in my father's words) not long for
this world, a dreamer;
That spirit running loose, that spirit running
free,
That spirit of hope, of jubilation and exultation,
That spirit of prophecy, not dying, come down
to us,
Going on — my brother and I, liberated, coveted,
being free.

And it shall speak in this our world.

And words are precious
And should not be flung away,
Not simply to the breeze —
Unless the day is breezy —
Just as a kiss is precious
And should not be left unkissed,
Nor a life unlived, not floating
away.

And women are the downfall,
So let a man turn his sight
From women and on the world.
For woman is a container,
A vessel to bear fruit,
So let a man comport himself
In such a way as to be deserving.
But lest he be too proud, too sure,
Let him remember that others
Can fill the vessel as well as he.

And this was my last tempest.
All save this had more to come,
And now, sailing into calm.

In the Biblical Style

And I came up out of Eilat
And my heart was sorely smitten.
And He bade me return across the sea —
And I did. I returned across the sea
And disembarked at Marseille,
Following the soft route of civilization:
Athens, Piraeus, the Peloponnesus,

Sicily, the boot of Italy,
The Straits of Messina, the Aeolian
Isles,
Stromboli, Naples, the lights of Rome,
Genoa, the Cote d'Azur — and I went
Along the Cote and I sought her out.
And the Lord was with me at night
upon the beach,
Succoured me, buoyed me up,
Watched over me when two thieves
Came along in the night to molest me —
woke me.
So I rose up and placed fear in their
hearts
Where before there had been stealth —
Two thieves and two rocks, a rock
for each,
And they went off down the beach
muttering.
And He watched over me when
I returned once more to sleep
With the night and the moon and
the sea,
And the following morning when I awoke,
a glorious morning.
And He provided lodging for me
The next two nights even unto Paris —
In the field at night and a ride upon
the road by day,
And I came back to this country,
The land of my ancestors, the land of
my forefathers,
And He watched over me in my trials,
Bore my waverings and misendeavors,
Waited while I floundered —
So He has succoured me, so I have
been succoured,
So He has blessed me, so I have
been blessed.

"Tonight the moon is full
And it goes with me" —
Give it up and grow,
And let the world imprint
itself upon you.

And this is what Paris has
meant to me,
And this is why I now am
free.
This is why I can go back
To pay my respects any time,
For what was proven there
Never needs a proof again —
Though perhaps renewal —
Never needs to be proven
elsewhere,
That a man can survive.
And though someone can go
One place and not another,
I can go all places and
survive.
This is Paris, the microcosm
of our universe —
All things concentrated there,
All things magnified there.

No more do I dedicate my life to a woman,
No more to one single being,
But now to all of men, to all of women —
some Higher Thing.

Why not,
Dear father?
Am I not but
A projection
Of thee?

And this is what the Monaco Cafe
has meant to me:
A place with the best of all possible
worlds and the worst,
The ugliest and the most noble —
Thieves, sidewalk artists, drink-grub-
bers, and brawlers;
And a place for the lovely,
The sensitive man and woman,
the ennobling.
And this is what I now have learned —
Once ventured, nevermore the urge,
Once all attempted, never again the
need,
Survival there, survival everywhere,
The best of al possible worlds
And the worst of all possible worlds —
In the sewers of Paris,
The coffee bars of London,
The deserts of North Africa,
The kibbutzim of Israel,
The subterranean world of New York
And the esotericism of India.

The Secret Musings of my Soul

I have pledged
My love to one.
I cannot pledge
It to another.

You know,
I cannot
Leave you.
Our souls
Are bound
Together.

Can I not take
You with me, love?
Why can I not take
You with me, love?

I am ready
Now to
Say farewell.

For now it is
I go into
The unknown.

Prayer upon Departure

The Lord is bountiful. Praise be His Name.
The Lord is merciful.
Praise Him with timbrel and harp,
Praise Him with lyre and song. Praise His
Name,

For He has wrought marvelous works.
His universe is good and He also.
The Lord is merciful, the Lord is good.
Praise Him for His wondrous ways.

The Lord protects my coming in and my
going out,
The Lord watches over me.
There is no fear, no trespass,
No thing, He does not understand.

Praise Him for His wondrous ways,
Praise Him with dancing and song.
How wonderful are His ways
They are good and righteous altogether.

How finite is infinity.

Aboard the *Liberte*

I fear I have
Lost her
For eternity.

And all
These things
Are chains.

These halls
Are hallowed
By her steps.

Heal, heart, heal.

These are the chains
That will not let
My spirit soar.

And so I went back.
And now I go on.

The Three Springs

There are three springs —
The spring of this world,
The spring of God,
And the spring of some other —
There is the Devil also in God's.
No matter how precarious
I go on drinking of God's.

On the Eve of Disembarkation

I leave your ghost upon this ship,
dear Barbara.

You cannot serve two fathers.

I have cast loose from
the shore.
The shore is of home
And love and country —
I hope the securing
line is held fast.

The Coat to Clothe
my Spirit in:

There are two coats.
This one seems to be
Of darkest silver;
That one, much richer,
Seems to be of gold.

And America is but a cloak,
And Israel, too, is but a cloak —
A journey, too, to India.
But there is no cloak there
Upon the soul laid bare.

I remember those words
On the day of parting:
"The soul is willing,
But the body not."

It shall have,
Of course,
To be Paris.

Yes, I tell thee,
Flee from me,
For I am suddenly
A child in darkness.

In such a chorus:
The journey
Of the soul
Through Hell.

I am in the winter of my soul.

Jerusalem and London

From Jerusalem to London,
A complete revolution of the earth,
A complete revolution of the seasons —
From light to dark, warm to cold,
summer to winter;
From Israel to England, a complete
revolution of the soul.

My soul pours forth in
Bold and sweeping strokes —
I shall write paeans to the Creator.

If this is to be, then,
A chronicle of darkness,
Let it be, then,
A chronicle of darkness.

I am looking into the abyss.
How can I rebuke thee?
If you had but once
Come to save me,
I would have been saved —
But instead, I am
Looking into the abyss.

The Monaco Cafe

I looked into the abyss and what did I see?
The Monaco Cafe, the pure unsullied soul of man.
People pass by and are afraid to look in.
Others are fascinated, hesitant, or are doubtful,
But always returning for a second look,
Peering through the glass partition at them.
This is why they run to their countesses for
protection;
The fear hangs over all. This is why these men
are so frightened —
They do not wish to face the forces of destruction
Mirrored there. This is why all the interactions.

Stranger, having looked through the window at these
lights,
Do not go in but close this book, for you have taken
this journey once before;
And whatever you build, build it not on such infirm
foundation,
For no beauty dwells there. Honour, courage,
affection, yes —

That is why Paris is the center and why there
Is no place like it in the entire physical universe.
And this is what my journey to Jerusalem and my
return to America meant —
And what my "Passage," too, "to India" will mean.

And all the conferences of the world are upon it,
Beauty afraid and innocence fleeing — Barbara, Nira,
The Scottish guitarist bemoaning his lost fame,
The penniless German sidewalk artists,
The Italian burned, a poor girl from Berlin,
The poet aside and watching,
The two witches from Copenhagen — one a
deformed leg,
The Nazi brute, the little English girls
And innocent and pugilistic English boys
Coming to Paris to test their masculinity;
The American girls, unsuspecting prey;
The blacks, the perverted G.I.,
The Peruvian — honour, a strength apart;
And Heather, some sturdy emotion;
The students, writers, artists, the innocent chatter,
The violence, the flatterers, the thieves: Hafid,
Benny, Big Fred;
Will, the killers, the Algerians —
The Monaco Cafe was the soul of this world laid bare,
Man bereft of all his endeavors —
And no beauty, no innocence residing there.

I looked into the abyss and I have been saved.
I have seen the darkest and the lightest —
I am no longer afraid.

I am not all my father,
Nor all my mother —
But a synthesis of the two.

Yes, and I have a right to speak,
For I am of the wandering Jew —
And I say unto you all,
Yellow man, black man, and white,
Be proud of your blood,
For this is what makes
You equal unto one another.

Put down your weapons,
All you peoples of the earth,
For the most marvelous time has come.
Lay down your mistrust, put down your fear,
For the most marvelous time has come.

Another moon and night.

Leicestershire in Winter

To Mr. Seton

If I could but break
Through unto your daughter, sir —
If I could do these things;
If I could only come into
Harmony with her cold exterior —
If I were so great;
Then I am sure I would find
Some giant loveliness there.

Heather Seton:

You are my sister that was not born
And I am your brother that was not born.
Hold up your head high, my girl,
There is blood between us.

Aphrodite

Do you smile on me tonight Venus,
The one bright star in all the sky?
Are you beside me once again, O Venus —
You in the clear and February sky
descending?
Do you hear the children playing,
Are you the same — the one the Greeks
call Aphrodite?

Venus in the Wintertime

The rows of chimney pots smoking,
The brick and silhouettes against the
sky,
The soft colors mingling at its base —
The clear bright sky at twilight,
And Venus constant over all.

Lines written on a Bridge in Brooklyn
— "to a Dying Love" —

Let me recreate those lines now,
Lines which should have been written
then —
A young man sitting on a bridge
In Brooklyn, and nothing happening;
A bright lovely, sunny autumn day,
With the leaves still yellow and not
yet gone,
Waiting for something to happen,
Wishing for something to happen,
Imagining something happening —
But nothing happening — not then, not
now, not ever.

Is love there now?
There is a soft memory
Of daisies and lilacs —
A velvet coverlet.

Take your hand
From about my heart.
You are constricting it.

The roses invariably
Pass into summer,
Spring inevitably
Wanders along,
Beauty passeth away —
A new thing cometh.

There is amethyst in the air,
All is covered in amethyst.

I do not understand it,
Not from the beginning
and not now.
I shall never understand it.

The Lord has lifted up my eyes,
The Lord has taken away my blindness.
Shadows dance in the supple sunshine,
Birds dart in the meadows — the meadows
are full,
Leaves reappear on the trees.
The world is alive with their sound.
The sun grows warm in the sky of my
rejoicing.

There has been
Much idolatry,
Much falsehood.

O thou of so little
faith
Can you not see?
The whole universe is
Spread out for thee.
Work a little today,
Do what thou must do.
Tomorrow there will be
Plenty of time to rest.

At Tilsbury Pier
April 4, 1961

I, too, have worked like you men
And wandered a thousand miles
        to set my spirit free.
I, too, have seen the derricks
And the cranes — the oil slicks,
Seen the fourth-month seagull soaring,
Smelt the smell of the sea.
I, too, have seen men working
Busily, day in and day out.
For what? To own, to create wealth —
To possess, for their own comforts.

On the Street in Amsterdam

Justice is not the word,
Force is not the word,
Power is not the word,
The word is Truth.

A Morality

And no thing freely given can be wrong —
No gift given freely that cannot be accepted,
No hospitality offered, no shelter given freely,
no alms without a string,
No food proffered genuinely that cannot be accepted.
And no action freely accepted that can be wrong,
No woman entered freely, no man accepting freely;
But if there was hesitation, if there is uncertainty,
If there was coquetry, if there needs be coaxing, if
there was seduction,
If the thing was tempted and the temptation accepted,
If there was a bribe, a motive — any gift, any
offering, any kiss,
Any hostage, any touch, any caress, any holding back;
Then is the thing not freely done, the gift not
freely given,
Then is the thing brought low, the act reduced in
Direct proportion to the deception, the seduction;
Then is the act made common in direct relation
To the amount held back, the amount held false —
In direct proportion to the thing not given.

The word has gone forth from Israel
Unto all the peoples of the earth.
I come to renew his word.
"You shall beat your swords into ploughshares
Your spears into pruning hooks,
And neighbor shall not rise up against neighbor,
Neither shall they learn war anymore,"
And the word shall be peace.

And European shall no longer smite European,
Neither shall he smite any other,
Nor any other smite him.
And Asian shall not smite Asian,
Nor African smite African.

And American shall not smite American.
Neither shall any Asian smite any African,
Neither shall he rise up against any other;
Neither shall any African rise up against any
Asian,
For His word shall be peace and His law shall
be just.

Neither shall you take anything
I say secondhand,
Nor out of the mouths of books,
Nor out of the mouths of babes,
Nor out of the mouths of fools.
Neither shall you take counsel
From any other or give counsel.

For the word that I speak is very nigh
And you shall commune with Me
directly,
For I am the Lord Your God
"And thou shalt have no other gods
before Me."

The Church? There is no Church.
There is only one God
And you shall worship in His Temple.

There is no
Other like You
In all the earth.

Once more at peace.

May 13th, 1961:

Crossing, once more, into Turkey
And the coming to the East.

I could write
Those poems again —
Every one again.

The same faces smiling,
The same children following,
The same great
White and black birds
(In rhythm with the tracks).

But this time I should
No longer be alone
And now the leaves are out.

I had a dream last night
And the dream was perfect.

The Crossing into Persia

The land of Cyrus,
The land of Xerxes.

The road is bumpy,
The road is long.

Great, green mountains
On either side
Ringing us in,
Turning into
Rock cliffs — stone.

Women sitting in
The field of trees —
And geese.

Carts with horses, children,
The donkeys with packs —
Bullocks too.

The first thing
Is to be
Completely clean.

Look at that nice smile —
Man with donkey
Almost hit.

Something moves me about
Going through these lands.

My companions in the bus:

Venice-hatted student,
Armenian, Israeli,
Persian officer,
Old man dying,
Merchant, soldier,
Musselman driver.

Long block
Houses of clay
Red in the sun.

There was a time —
And it was then —
When I was welcome
Wherever I went —
And it shall come
again.

A horseman
Alone
On the desert.

There was a time
When I wrote
Very lovely poems —
And something happened,
I begin to write again.

Let the Persian boy
Sleep upon your
Shoulder.

The land is great,
The land is massive,
The land is greater
Than its people.

Shadows upon the land,
Green fields
And brown.

Herds of camels
And cattle running.

Men spread out over the
plains.

There is land to step upon.

I know that Voice,
And listen to it
And follow it.

"Take off
Your glasses,
For you shall
Find sight."

I shall be recreated again
In Your image
And cross
A thousand deserts.

Oasis Poems

A Man on a bicycle,
A man walking by the road —
I chronicle my journey.

A man ploughing by the side,
Donkeys with hay,
The sound of the horn,
Music jangling.

I take these things
Out of the desert.
I repaint myself.

Behold!
Thou shalt not perfume me,
Not with perfume or myrrh.
I bring my own odour into
the world.

In Teheran

On Changing Direction
for the Peace Corps:

You cannot fill a hole
By throwing dirt in it.
It is like sand running
From beneath a breach.
You can fill it only by
Overstepping, ignoring,
or forgetting it.

Of all the people whom I love,
I still love her the most —
It must be her mouth.

The tears
That hang
On the edge
Of my eyes.

In Flight

I took the silver bird
And traced an arc
Across the sky.

Do the clouds fall down?
Why then the plane?

And the Lord gave me sight.

On meeting a
Roman going home:
Every land calls its own.

Up the Adriatic to Rome

My whole life
Is opening up before me
Like a rolling green pasture.

I want first
To discharge
My obligations
To my homeland.

My heart is soaring.

I have no right to be happy,
Nothing to hope for,
Yet it is so.

Into the Western sun.

With the Peace Corps in
Berkeley, California:

It is not for me here to
be.

On Stinson Beach

And sometimes, when
Walking along the beach,
One comes upon a shell
And, picking it up, one
Sees the shell is empty —
The creature has moved on.

I have learned certain rules,
But the rules are not these.
There was a place, but the place
is not here.
I saw a sea, but the sea is no more,
"There was a dense forest and
Suddenly the trees fell down."

I have walked numerous miles,
But the way is now gone.
There was a time, but the time
is not now,
There were some words, but the
words are not these,
There is a way, but the way is
sometimes lost,
There is a Voice, but it is
Not to be sacrificed like this.

Forget My voice
Until you can
Utter it at peace.

Poetry is the voice
Of the fields.
Are you so weak?

This is no time
For easy living.

I have done
What I have to do here.
Now I must rejoin my people.

Paris, August 14th, 1961

These are the bonds
That tie a man down.

Wisdom is aged.

I believe in a dream.

PART THREE

ON THE HILLS OF NORTHERN PALESTINE

1961

Crete

The clouds which almost touch
The top of the hills,
The red and green,
The brown speckled with shrub,
The light blue sky,
The soft hills —
The island sitting full black
In the evening sun.

Israel:

I could have embraced
This land when I came —
The land of my fathers.

It is not I
Who have
Strayed,
Dear father.
I shed
These tears
For you.

How salty
The tears
Are here.

To Have Come Back

I have seen the clouds
come over the land,
I have seen Hermon in
cloud.
I have breathed the dust.
I have seen the grass
in the Huleh
Bend with the wind, and
the trees.
I have heard the drops
in the darkness.
I have stood and seen
The side of the valley
Slope away into Lebanon,
the sheets of rain.
I have touched the fish,
I have touched the grapes.
I have felt the young men
beside me sure-footed.
To have come back —
The tears leave stains
Upon my shirt and drip
From the edges of my eyes.

I have felt rain in
the Holy Land —
Holy rain.

I stopped work for the Sabbath in
October when the rains came.

I am drunk
with it,
I cannot get
Enough of it.

By the Sea of Galilee:

A man must have a way
As strong as the land around him,
That can withstand the winds,
Lay motionless in the midday sun,
And drink up water beneath the storms.

First Joseph read it
And passed it on to —
Then Moses read it
And passed it on to —
Then David read it
And passed it on to —
Then Solomon read it
And passed it on to —
Then the Prophets
read it.

On thinking of Iran:

There you were
Free and running.
There was no way
Of jumping over it
And going on to India.

How happy I was then.
Lord replenish my soul.
There is this pain. Take
it away.

And all the sins I have been forced
to commit,
All the flaws that have come out —
All the faults and all the weaknesses,
all the cracks.
And I was not going to bring them with me
But I carry them here within my heart —
All those days that led nowhere,
All those indecisive moments,
But there is no other land to expiate
them in.

On Coming up to Jerusalem
A Triumph to Celebrate my Return

To have come back,
To have wound
The way wound
So many ages ago,
Up through the round
And flattened hills,
The grey and stucco
Houses climbing.
Sing my heart.
Hear, O Lord,
Proclaim a celebration.
I am in Jerusalem
And the long way
is done.

November 3rd, 1961 — Jerusalem

The wonders I have seen
This day are beyond belief.
I have seen a rainbow
Spanning the Old City
From one end to the other.
I have seen rain in pellets
Falling angrily upon the
Streets of the New City.
I have seen water running
In torrents down the old
Cobblestone streets.
I have seen hail bouncing
Like golf balls amid the
puddles.
And I have dreamed dreams,
Oh I have dreamed dreams —
An oath upon King David's
tomb —
I have seen a rainbow
Cupping the Old City pre-
senting it to me

My eyes have confounded me,
My heart has deceived me.
I have seen things I ought
not to have seen.
Yet still I believe.

On overlooking the edge
of the city and burning
the sweater knitted for
me by my cousins:

I tell you I could have
Spared you all your pain.
I promise you there would
have been no pain
Had you but listened to My
Voice.

She could not have lived very long.
I was fortunate to have had her when I did.
And after that, there would have only been
The man grown tall, the man grown strong —
An Eisenman — but oh, to have her now,
Upon my body, upon my chest, next to my skin.
But if one cannot, then one cannot
And it was better not to have gone.
Better to have stood firm
And, if you cannot, then do not —
Better to do nothing than do a thing badly,
Better say nothing than say a thing badly.

And now? I am in the right direction,
Like a man walking precariously,
Like a man walking nervously,
But walking all the same — sometimes slowly,
Sometimes more rapidly, at the highest steadily,
Not to look back, not to be turned round
To the right or the left but walking straight,
Not a business, not a pleasure — but to carve *a thing.*

Bless me Lord, for I am Your son.
Bless me Lord, for I stand before You as I once
stood when I was a boy.
Bless me Lord, for I knew much for young
years.
I stand before You that boy — tall, lean, my
spirit easy.
Bless me Lord, for I am Yours. My heart has
come around to You —
That in me has been tempered, prepared for
You.
Bless me Lord, cause my right arm to be
strong;
My left hand, a touch; my heart to be lithe;
My limbs to answer evenly; Your mercy to be
upon me;
Cause me to deal justly, my arm not to tremble,
My spirit not to waiver, my step to be even,
My spirit not raucous, my lips not to talking,
My brain not to soften, cause my fingers to be
tender,
My soul to be health — my being to be mine.

As hard as it has been for me,
So will it be for
The Children of Israel to speak My Name.
As much as I have gone through,
So will they have to go through,
Before the earth opens
And their children begin to sing.

The Lord shall hit you
So that one by one,
You slap your heads
And say, "I know that He
is."

The Lord watches over me,
The Lord is my shepherd,
The Lord sees my every touch,
The Lord makes my soul to sing,
The Lord makes my body leap like
a spring lamb.
The Lord is my shield,
The Lord is my right arm.

Sasa

My spirit reawakens.
It is the way of
All things.

The words are
Not yet ripe —
They do not come.

Son of Man,
Go out from
Among the people.

A man can have
No friend —
It must be the Lord.

He did not place man
Upon this earth
To pollute it
With his weaknesses.

To my Cousins:

The Lord has brought a curse
upon you
Because you received me
And then received me not.
Your father's house has He
brought low
And all who dwell therein.
Your lives has He cut short,
Your dreams, your hopes, your
house
Has He made an abomination.
He has brought sickness upon
you,
He has brought death.
He has made you heinous
Unto one another's sight.
He has made you two-faced,
He has made you petty.
Your daughters has He made
barren
And caused no seed to come
forth,
Because you received me
And then received me not —
Because you took my happiness
And gave it to a stranger.

Thou has taken away my love,
Given her to another,
Polluted her —
Yet still I want her.

Lord, return her to me —
She is the State of Israel,
She has wandered after
Foreign gods, been polluted,
Yet still I want her back.

You made a donkey of yourself
Braying at the moon.
When you turned away from
The way of the Lord,
You became a fool.

See you daughters of Jerusalem,
See you sons of Zion,
See how the Lord mocks you
In your hour of deliverance.
See how you are made beggars
Even on your day of triumph.
See you camped upon the hills
Outside the walls of the Old City —
Your tents spreading down
The slopes of the New City
Clinging as if by a thread
To the Mountain of Zion,
Which the Lord has given you
As a sign that He is still with you,
Though you turn away from Him,
Laugh at Him, mock Him in your
empty lives.

Many voices have I heard
All going separate ways,
Many voices and many ways —
All is vanity, vanity, vanity.

And Israel has returned
But where is Judah?
The land still remains unclaimed
And already you turn aside.

On the Hills of Northern Israel

I set off this morning early,
Nothing but myself alone,
Walking through the hills
Of Northern Israel.

I saw a boy talking and with sheep,
I saw the Arab village on top the hill,
I saw Mt. Hermon in the background.

A boy talking and with sheep,
The Arab village on top the hill,
Mt. Hermon in the background,
The braying of sheep,
The sound of the wind
Whirring off the empty hills,
The sound of my feet pouncing
On the concrete of the road,
The swish of my pants,
My belt jangling,
The wind pressing against my ears —
A sparrow, a crow —
The mountain alone on my right,
The red of Lebanon,
The villages speckled,
The sun bright in
The heavens of the sky.
The empty whistle of a bird,
The piles of dung along the road,
The brown fields lying fallow,
The tit of a sparrow,
A car coming down out of the slope —
A butterfly — the green shoots of
grass,
The sound of a hawk, a fly,
Rocks strewn over the hills —
The needle being sown together,
The dogs coming running, barking,
The boys sitting with the sheep.
I am whole.

In the Christian Arab village of *Geesh*
(Gush Halav), on seeing the pamphlet
on the Holy Shroud:

And the rains cleared —
The lights of Sasa,
The lights of Safad.

I started out afraid.
Then I forgot
Everything around me.

Enjoy the life
Wherever you
Find it.

In the Arab village
at night:

You must never
Be afraid
Again.

Morning in Nazareth

Smells of Greece —
The sun, the people,
The carts, the markets,
The church, and him.

I have heard
The cock crow
In Nazareth.

I ask you not to read
The bible like religious men,
But to read it to know
What sort of men you are,
So you will know from where
you came
And why you have come back,
So you will not be petty,
Nor walk with heads bent low —
So you will be noble,
So your minds will be open,
Your souls be richer —
So you will not push and shove
On line while waiting for the bus,
So you will not rob or cheat,
But rather, treat each other with
consideration.

I did not work well today —
I will work well and smooth
like a knife,
I will do the things on this
earth,
Well and smooth like a knife,
I will work in the fields,
Well and smooth like a knife,
I will work by the day, in the
night,
By the way, in the sea —
Well and smooth like a knife.
I will plant, I will reap,
I will tread upon this earth
And enter into the company
of men,
Well and smooth like a knife.

What of Samaria?

What of Samaria, what of
Jericho, Heshbon, and Hebron?
What of all those lands still
held captive?
Have you come back for naught,
Have you come back to dwell
At the edge of the sea?
Galilee yes and Sharon — the
desert
Even unto the edge of the sea.
But what of your Fathers' Lands —
What of the edge of the Jordan?

Thoughts on the bus going
up to Haifa:

Where is He?
He is not sitting by the way,
Nor walking along the road.

The Christian Arab and
the Druse

The Lord has certainly
Made them strong,
But why has He made
The Christian Arab,
The Druse, finer, better —
Not so mean, petty, or
ungodly?
And why do I like
These others better?
What have we in common?

The Arabs and the Druse

O Lord, why do you divide us so?
Why are we one nation and they another,
Yet both of the same people?
Why is it their music I love — their spirit?
Why do you test me so?

There is a delicate line —
If you listen to it,
It is the only way to live.

There is a way —
That way is easy,
That way is certain,
That way is even,
That way is straight.

O Children of Israel:

The word has been taken out from you,
The word and the spirit, and is no longer yours.
The Lord has poured out His wrath upon you
And dispersed you unto all the countries of the earth.
For two thousand years He has made you strangers
upon the earth,
Caused your bones to fill the valleys, the mountains,
Burned your bodies, turned them to ash, incinerated
them —
And He has risen you up. He has gathered you up
From all the nations of the earth and returned you
to this land.
He is not hard-hearted, He is not merciless,
He has made good His promise unto Jacob.

But as a sign that He has found you no better than
your neighbors,
He has taken away the beauty of His voice —
The voice of His prophets has He caused to become
still.
No longer shall there be prophets,
No longer shall His voice reside among you —
Yours which was His most precious gift, you His
chosen,
To you no longer belongs His choice — His voice.
And as a sign, too, that He has retracted His gift,
He has made you like any other nation —
The Jews as the Egyptians and the Syrians,
The Jews as the English, the French,
The Jews as the Americans — as you wish to be.
His radiance, His voice, has He taken out from
among you.

And as a sign that, though He has gathered you up
And brought you back to this land,
He has found you no better than your neighbors,
He has placed you under the authority of the
Council of Nations,
Where you wish to be, free of the burden of His
choice.
So has He freed you.

And as a sign, too, that His word has gone out from
among you,
His city, the City of David — Jerusalem, has He
withheld from you.
He has brought you back and given you once more
the land
He promised unto Jacob, but His city, His chosen,

His rejoicing,
Which you made unclean with your unfaithfulness,
He has withheld from you as a sign that He still
Takes great pleasure from its presence on the earth.
And as a sign, too, that you shall dwell in peace, no
more His Chosen,
He has made you as your neighbors — now one of
the peoples of the earth.

A Lamentation for the lustre of Israel which has
gone out,
A lamentation for the glory of Israel which shall
be no more,
A lamentation for the priests, the prophets, the
poet-kings.
Weep you mountains, cry you winds, for the beauty
of Israel
Which shall be no more — weep for the sweetness
of the lute
Which shall no more be heard in the tents of your
rulers.
Weep you mountains, weep o rocks, mourn you
stones,
Skip no more ye lambs, for the radiance of Israel
which has gone out.

No more are you His Chosen People —
So now be at peace, you Children of
Israel.

He has caused His voice
To go out from among you.
The word has gone out from Israel.
His word has gone forth
In the mouths of men —
I come to renew His word.

And I am cold.

Son of Man,
Go out from this place.
Tomorrow, go and stand
On the edge of the earth.

Snow on Mt. Hermon

Snow on Mt. Hermon,
Clouds upon the hills.
A cold rain that comes
in sweeps,
A white moon at night,
And lights of towns to
guard my sleep.

Three or four more days
And the time here
Will be accomplished.

I have seen
The caps
Of Lebanon in snow.

To Climb a Hill

A blue sky and wisps of cloud,
The red of Lebanon, the town,
Mt. Hermon, Kibbutz Sasa, and
the hills around,
Green fields and the blue moun-
tains of Syria.
A vulture in the sky, wings spread
and white head,
Mount Carmel, Haifa, the blue
Mediterranean — Lebanon is red.
Northern Israel cupped within
my hands.

On thinking of
"the Beat Poets" smoking
pot by the Sea of Galilee:

They bring their
Own earths with them.
I walk next to the sky.

I am here,
Not to
Go to India,
But to
Know Israel.

From where I have come:

To stand at the end
Of the Mediterranean
And look out to the West,
Canaan south and Lebanon
        north,
The east in Syria,
The cradle of the world.
To see what times
Have now been come —
        what lands.
To sit on top of a hill
And peer out over to the
        sea —
The peoples of the earth,
        their source.

My twenty-fourth year,
After much travail,
I stood upon the hills
Of Northern Palestine
And looked out towards
barren Syria.

To kneel upon the
earth,
To see the ancient
towns,
To feel the wind.

I was not
Making love
To woman.

Walking upon the land
With blue mountains
And a song.

The Lord is in the
sky.

A grove of
Olive trees,
The clear sky.

There is much
I have to know,
Much happiness,
Much freedom,
With them and
every man.

By my twenty-fifth year,
I walked into the life
I wanted to live.

Like the
Connecting
Pieces of a rod.

My people are the whole earth.
Then do not say it —
Let it be.

Change
Is
The essence
Of all things.

On the bus leaving Kibbutz Sasa:

We are all actors,
Dancers around
A pole.

Somewhere
Along the way
I shall meet,
Now — then,
a woman

There is a way.

On the Bus

We are all here
For a time
In the same pit.
Therefore,
It is necessary to
Treat each other
With consideration.

In the Emek

You must have nerve.

I shall know women.

Kibbutz Hazorea —
under the lights
of the chicken coop:

He enjoys his own being.

Tel Aviv in Rain

Coming out
Of the storm —
And now, soft breezes.

On Thinking of the Cafes
in Vienna:

They are all going home.
The pull is too great.

On a Post-office Bench
in Jerusalem:

To see a black man in
Jerusalem,
Multi-colored cap
Upon his head and
Sweater tossed jauntily
Back over his shoulder —
Red, black, yellow, and blue.
He does not belong and yet,
It is good that he is here —
New countries, a touch —
Something will grow.

On seeing the American in
the Tourist Office:

Why? Because he has money,
So they fleece him;
And yet,
He wants to be fleeced.

On Sasa:

What was there
is
No more there.

On finding a job building:

Build beneath it and around
it,
And it will be constructed.

If one thing is lost,
A new thing is found.

There are different ways
When a man is moving,
When a man is stopped.

You store up
Your strength
In your work,
And then
You let it out
In your talk.

It is like
The piles of rocks
At a building site —
One day there are
Only a few stones left
And one must be careful.
Each one is precious.
But the next day,
A new load arrives
And one can proceed
more easily.

I love this life.
It is as it should be.
When a man has no
work,
He is down. When he
Finds a job, he is up.
For these moments
It could not be better.

I sleep where I want,
I eat when I want.
There is nothing to fear —
Inside one is sometimes lost.

What money?
I do not need money.
It is better to feed
One's soul on the moon.

On money:

I do not
Need it,
Not now,
Not ever.

On my sleeping bag, blanket,
and clothes:

I have only you now.

PART FOUR

THE CUP OF TREMBLING

1961

In the Convent de St. Isaie

The Key

It is golden,
It fits the lock,
It opens the door.
One walks up the path,
Through the olive trees —
The moon, the night,
The light in the sky —
One enters the Convent.

Here is the key
To the Church.
If you want to,
enter.

Tomorrow,
Do not go
And do not
Build either.

The next day supersedes
The one before —
There are many jobs.

Time, time, time to do it slowly.
The slower it is done,
The better it will be done.

To make a man welcome
Is the charge of the host.
He succeeds in the freedom
he offers.
He does not in so far as
The restrictions he imposes —
His conduct is the thing.

The coming
Of the New Year
Crosses out missteps.

There is no fear
That it will stop,
No worry — it has come.

On thinking of Paris:

If they played their guitars
        upon the streets,
I shall play a different song.

My brother
Is an architect —
He has nothing on me.

I have come a long way.

On thinking
of my cousins
in Jerusalem:

This is
My house,
Not that one.

I do not
Any longer
Know who I am.

In the Convent
de St. Isaie,
Jerusalem:

I am lost to you.

O Lord, give me
The power to be
Someone you love.

I do not worry
For a bed
To sleep, to eat —
These things come.

The word is powerful.

Christian Poems

If "The Man is the Word"

If "the man is the word" —
The words of Pere Jacques —
Then it is much greater
Than previously I thought.
Then is he greater, Moses
greater, and
The Church, though upheld
By imperfect men, greater.
Then is he the king,
The government, the world.

Have you ever been to a Catholic service —
Do you see the poetry in it?
Men pay homage to something higher
Than the Lord of Hosts.

There is poetry in Catholicism —
The soul with the body,
The spirit with the Law.
There is symbolism and there are acts —
There is corruption, there is grace.

Christianity is the
Complement of Judaism.
Can you compare Jesus
With the Rabbis?
Jesus was my brother.

This people do not know the Lord —
And that people do not know 'Jesus.'

There is something missing here.
There is a thing which is not here —
A feeling, a touch, a blessing, a choice.
To find it, one must go back to the beginning.

To Father Bruno:

I am sorry
For my words of
The other night.
They come from
Some imperfect
Understanding.

Christianity is the flower of Judaism.
Christianity is poetry —
How simple.
John preached forgiveness
Of sin in the wilderness.
Don't you see what Judaism flowered into,
The resurrection of the soul —
It is pure poetry.
Do not tell me about the other Christians,
Do not tell me about the English,
The Romans, the French.
I am a Jew —
I knew what it was
To be a "Christian" before they.

Who am I — I will tell you.
I am one of the first Christians.
I am of the blood of Peter, James, and Paul.
Their blood is my blood;
Their religion, my religion.

Without Christianity Judaism is not complete.
Neither is Christianity without Judaism, the body and the soul.
The Jews, who were the Chosen People, needed to cling to
Their incompleteness in order to return. Otherwise, they would Have disappeared.

And now to be reunited, the body with the soul.
A great house will be built, an everlasting union.
And now that the Jews have returned, both may go on together.
"Peter" will for the first time be "built upon rock."
All the religions of the earth will be imbibed.

"Jesus," who is he?
He is not what other men have said he is.
One cannot believe the reports.
To find him one must go back to the beginning,
To find him is to correct the mistakes,
To find him is to bring him back into the world,
To find him is to correct the wrongs
That have been done and said in his name.

In what way are you deserving of this land?
Because you have been outcasts, because you suffered much,
Because you have been lower than any race on earth? Is
this enough?
Do you think two thousand years is enough time in Heaven
to buy some land?
Do you deserve it More than the Arabs?
Is there not some excellence, some spiritual uprightness
Which the Lord has seen, that He has been so generous?

O Palestine, what love I of you?
Abraham, Isaac, and Moses,
Jesus, the Apostles, Paul,
The land —
I love nothing more.

On comparing them
with my professors:

There is a clearness
Even in those who
Cannot see.

What a pleasure it is
Not to hear the voices of my youth,
But to hear the voices of other countries.

Is this what
I have been
Coming towards
My whole life?
The saviour,
The creator,
The divine?

His spirit is upon
me,
His spirit is in me.

I am coming close,
My legs are crossed,
He is in my hand,
He is in my body.
The power of this thing
Is unbelievable —
The power for good
And the power for evil.

I am of the blood of Peter,
I am of the people of Paul,
I am of the word that
Was taken out of Israel
In a foreign tongue.
I keep that tongue,
For it is the word
And not the tongue. It is
both.

You shall
Grow to be
An old man.

On a Rooftop in the Morning in Jerusalem

I stood upon a rooftop
Looking out at the morning
And the sun was cool,
And I heard a guitar playing
And with it, after a time,
A woman's voice —
Perhaps Spanish, perhaps American.
And the door was open
With the window.
Who waited for me behind
That dark screen,
Those yellow stones? I wondered,
Should I enter?
No, the time was not yet right.
Not now — I went on.

To the Orders:

The time is coming when
You will have to choose
Between the Church
And the Holy One of Israel.

On reading Paul:

"There shall come
Out of Zion
The Deliverer"
(Romans 11:26)

Now that you have something
To say to this people,
You must go out upon the streets.

I bring with me
The salvation of the Jewish people:
In two words, "Jesus Christ."
Believe on him and you shall be saved.

You are but
A cup for
The word.

I come from the blood of John,
The blood of Peter,
The blood of Christ.
This blood has He made Holy.
Fortunate are they
To have our voices with them,
For we shall tell them things:
"Believe in Him,"
"Turn the other cheek," and
"Give thy cloak too."
The Church also will be made
to see.

The Church?
The hell with the Church.
They have kept "Jesus" in name only.

They have not been understood.
For centuries they have been speaking
In words that have not been understood.

They shall break out with the Voice
When they are called in one stroke.
Like an army at the sound of a bugle,
they shall come.

Before planting,
You must prepare
The earth very well.

No "Jesus" was right in coming.
The Jewish religion had not flowered till his
coming.
In the name of "Jesus Christ," "I forgive you
your sins",
Not in the name of the Catholic Church.
Before it was only a blind narrow road leading
nowhere but to him,
"A straight way in the wilderness" —
A path of blindness leading directly to him.
Those who are still upon it are but reflections
of its blindness.

But mock not, ye Christians,
For remember the words of my brother Paul
And hold your peace for, as certainly as
You are on the tree, you too can be removed —
If you have not already removed yourselves.
The tree is the tree of life and no man is
too lowly —
No man holds an honored or dishonored place
upon it.

Mock on,
Laugh,
Grovel,
You pigs!

On not having children:

It was not through me
That I came to be.
I have not the right
To partake of it all myself.
(The sin of my mortality).

O Lord,
Help me to be
Someone You love.

It comes like a waterfall, a flood —
Wonderful to be a man,
Master of one's self —
In control.

The Promise

Yes, you have come back
And now you are the Land's,
Strong, sun-baked, weather-beaten.
You are like a cup awaiting the wine,
You are a body, a strong hillside,
And water shall be poured upon you.
You shall be anointed
And the vessel shall run over.

It is like playing
A guitar on the streets —
I gave my guitar away.

On my brother's friend
Elizabeth's death:

So it begins.

On Father Jacques' words:

It is quite possible they shall be
Pushed into the sea a second time
And the Lord shall bring them back
a third time —
Not these. There are six million in
America,
Six million motherless, homeless,
hopeless.
The Lord has not forgotten them;
And they shall bring it back
Full of hope and spirit — the New
Land —
And plant His banner in Jerusalem.
It is possible they shall come back
a third time —
Two thousand years are not yet done —
With renewed hope and love. Why not?
I don't think so.

Tomorrow,
I go down
Into the desert.

The words
Carve
The way.

I want to be everywhere
At once in this country.

Have you ever stepped out so
That tomorrow is uncertain?

The Lord has made me
Welcome upon the land —
everywhere.

On Seeing Bethlehem in Cloud and
Listening to the Young Men with
Machine Guns Speaking Hebrew:

I feel a wind coming out of Bethlehem —
There are no "Jews" anymore.
You either must come to Israel
Or become Christian.
Either way, you shall have to follow.

One comes
Into
The center
Of the world.

On Coming into the Center
of the World:

I see Jerusalem in cloud,
A cold wind blowing.
To see these things —
The Holy Ghost is upon me —
The wonder of them,
They cannot be lost.
There is a Church to hold it,
However imperfect the
vessels of men.

My eyes
Have seen
Bethlehem.

On the bus:

I feel the Holy Spirit is upon me.
"We are in something special.
Children of Israel, rejoice!"

On meeting the Oxford-
Educated, Jewish Boy
from India, "Joshua"
who said he was "Jesus":

He is the lost sheep
 of Israel,
He does not see yet —
He is not certain.
I cannot hold him
Upon my shoulders.

I do not serve
Men's ways —
I serve God's.

Ein Karem

In the Crusader Chapel
of John the Baptist

I am a voice crying
In the wilderness,
"Make My pathways straight."

The Day of my Crowning

That's twice today
The Holy Spirit was upon me:
Once with the children on the bus
And once in the chapel with the nuns.

The smell of the chapel —
Like heavy perfume,
Not cold and dank like Europe,
But full of the Crusades —
Yellow like the Holy Land
and blue.

On Seeing the Crusader Seal
in the Chapel with the Crown
Denoting "King of Men":

The Democracies have
Not yet learned,
Men are not kings.

Men forget how or from where
And then one day it comes —
They come soon.

The Lord hath told me
To come to John's
birthplace
To be baptized.
I don't know by whom —
Someone tomorrow.

The Eichmann Trial has some meaning
And Ben Gurion in Rangoon —
A Buddhist monastery.
All things have some meaning,
All things revolve,
All things come home.
My brother has some meaning,
My mother, my father —
All things — my voice, my touch.

On seeing a cross:

I am at peace with you,
O Jesus Christ.

I am not a wonder-worker,
Miracles I cannot do.

I have a mission to revive
the Jews.

Have you ever stepped out
So that tomorrow was
Uncertain?

If you believe in the Lord, then you need
not fear.
If you believe in some Higher Thing,
Then the workings of men upon this earth
Can have no affect on you.
You can turn the other cheek
Or take off your coat — it doesn't matter.
If you believe not, you cannot.
If you believe, it has no bearing
What another man does to you —
What pain you suffer has no bearing.

However, this is only belief.
It is not a doctrine for all men —
You cannot ask other men to follow this.
Supposedly he followed it and it was well
for him,
But not for others. This was his sin. He used
his power wrongly.
It is a natural thing, of course, the quest
for no fear.
He should have been king not crucified —
Both are now the same.

They who give me food,
They who give me sleep,
He who gives me his bed,
Who is my shepherd?

To be baptized,
Not into a Church,
Not by man,
But as a follower of Jesus,
Some sign to place upon me —
His word.

I have a thirst.
Now I am
Becoming filled.

He said it.
I do not have to —
I shall do it.

In the Convent of Notre Dame de Sion

Rain in the Convent garden,
Lights upon the hill,
On the slopes of Jerusalem,
A bright mist, a touch —
Outside the city,
Down in the valley,
A cold wind blowing.

His voice is
On the mountains —
A light to the world.

Now is the time.
If not now —
Then never.

On seeing the
monastery
in mist:

I did not go on.

This I will do for Jesus.
I will suffer it.
I want to be baptized
In the name of
John the Baptist and Jesus —
A son of Abraham, Isaac, and Jacob.

On seeing the clouds hovering over the hills,
The light beneath them,
The hills barren, green and brown,
The yellow gates of the convent — Jerusalem.

It is the feeling
Which is true —
Only this.
The touch changes it.

The walk is
Yellow golden.
It takes me
On the way.

I was on my way
To the desert
When suddenly
I stopped by here.

On thinking of last year in England:

"The Journey of the Soul through Hell."

To the Mother Superior:

I do not join armies,
I shall not do this service,
I shall not cry upon the streets,
Yet shall they hear me.

The wind is blowing,
The clouds are blue.

I was blessed one time,
Now is the second time.
I was blessed once —
Now I have come back.
The third time I come
I do not know
What there will be.

There is the cloud upon the hill
And the triangular light,
The round window of the hostel
And the top of the tree.

On the Path Walking
up to the Convent

Lord, you teach me
To bow down.
I do things
Very imperfectly.
I stumble,
I kneel down,
There is ceremony
And why not?
A moment's hesitation,
A state of grace —
Tomorrow there will
be more.

It is like being
In a great building
And only being able
To see down the corridors,
And there are no other choices.
Nothing on earth is high enough
for heaven,
Not buildings, not skyscrapers,
Not even the Church —
They are the work of the Devil:
"Get thee behind me Satan."

How many souls have been sold
To "the Devil" in false hope?
How many pitiably lost
On the final deathbed?
It is not in this world —
This world is "the Devil."

To do a thing blessedly, every act —
This is magic.
It is a kind of Christian charity.
This is a powerful thing.
Like this, there is nothing
You cannot have (I cross out lies).

The Convent Dining
Room

They have prepared
A table before me,
My cup runneth over.
Now that I am here,
I sit down as if to
a feast.
I am well served.

On thinking of
last year:

I lost my way
And so I lost
my girl.

You see the
rain
Has stopped.
It is clear —
A rainbow!

I looked up,
For one moment,
A rainbow —
Then it is gone.

On Seeing
the Monastery
atop the Hill:

There is
Something
I want
From there.

In the rain:

The Lord has blessed me.
I shall be both
Christian and Jew.

To Joshua — the Oxford Indian
Jewish boy, who thought wrongly:

I shall not forget you Joshua,
Nor your mournful cry.
The Jews shall not be forgotten.
There shall be hope.

I shall wait
Till I am summoned.
I shall not join the Church.

On the brother who
  said he was abbot:

I shall rise up men
Who tell words
That are true —
From the Lord!

On Joshua:

It is not he.
Neither is
It his name.

On viewing
the image
of Mary:

No baptism —
Not now,
Not ever.

To the Franciscans:

Vous n'etes pas, messieurs,
  comme St. Francis.

For me it is the same thing,
To be refused businesses,
To be refused baptism,
To be refused a job.
They are all churches —
And the men who run them.

The Catholics are they
Who have lost their shepherd —
He was their center,
The object of their faith,
And now it is their Church —
For me it is *the Lord*.

The madness beginneth,
The madness endeth.

I have not to go down into the desert.
I shall live by my Father's hand —
Neither have I to do any vain act.

Moon over Jerusalem,
Wind upon the hills,
Tomorrow I rest.

I have nothing to say to this people,
nor any people.
I have only to enjoy the earth,
The trees, the sky — some men.

The stars are out.
Tomorrow is a new day,
Tomorrow I want to sleep.

On reading Isaiah 49:16
("A Deliverer shall
arise from Zion"):

And the Lord said,
"I will not forget you.
Behold, I have engraven you
Upon the palms of My hands.
Your walls are continually
before Me."

No, I will not forget you.
Though you have sinned,
Though you have forgotten Me.,
Though you have been blind
and lost like sheep,
Though you have been as if
in sleep,
The Lord, thou lovest, still
loveth thee.
When you lift up your eyes —
your spirit,
Then shall you once more
His Chosen still be.

The Lord has not forgotten Israel.
Be not proud, you nations of the earth.
Though He remembers you,
He has not forgotten His Chosen Israel.

I looked up
And there was snow.
Just at that moment,
Snow white and pure,
Amid the rain, upon
the land —
White snow and light!

Snow in Jerusalem

It came with a sudden wind.
One moment there was none,
Then it had come — a darkness
and then the light.
Then it was gone like yesterday's
rainbow.

The Lord has said,
"*You are My People.*"
What He has said,
No *man* can take away.

There is
No baptism.
It comes only
From the Lord.

The Lord has chosen.
Bow down, bow down.
Yea, Lord — here!

Behold,
I have taken
Out of your hand
The Cup of Trembling.

Saturday Evening
in the Broken-down
Jewish Cafe in Ein Karem:

I am happy to be back
Among my own people.
Give me the vice,
Give me the filth,
Give me the dirt.

On seeing the pious nuns,
Heads bent low to
His wind:

They are not His servants —
no, Lord, no.
We worship Him in the fields,
in the sea.
We are all His servants,
We worship Him everywhere —
On the hills, in the mountains,
in the cities.
I bring tidings of great joy,
I bring tidings of great rejoicing.

On seeing
A line
To my brother:

I have no money,
I have His coat,
I have only joy.

I have received the blessing
from my father
And I shall not forget it:
"You shall be happy no matter
What passes or what comes.
You have it in you to persevere,
To be happy — and your brother,
not."

On "*Beulah*"

And it shall be
From the Lord, a name —
An everlasting sign
That you shall not be cut off.

They serve something
that is dead,
That has come and gone —
This is a new thing.

The Lord shall have mercy upon
Israel.
"Take up the stumbling block
Out of the way of My people"!
"There is no peace," saith the Lord
to the wicked —
"For My House shall be called
A House of Prayer for all Peoples."

On leaving Ein Karem

The Lord has risen me up.

The oranges are out —
The oranges and lemons
After the storm.

The Lord has taken me down
from Jerusalem.
To come down is very nice.

I serve the God of my fathers,
The God of Abraham, Isaac, and Jacob —
"Take up the stumbling block
Out of the path of My people"! —
The God of David and Jesus, not their
"Church."

Jaffa

The
Mediterranean,
I love it.

Jerusalem
Was clear
When I left.

Palm trees
And soft
Breezes.

The Lord said, "Not yet.
When you come back,
I tell you."

Sophie

You were seduced by "the Devil,"
"The Devil" came along and took
you away.
How else did she know you?
You should have known from her
face
Which was like the other's —
fool you.

And the Voice spoke,
"Tomorrow you go
Anywhere —
You love Him."

The lighthouse, the stars,
The palm trees, the moon,
The sky, the sea, the soft
breezes.

Jerusalem is
The center
Of the earth.
It all comes
From there.

Even the breakers are muffled.

On the 'Artists' entering the *Omar Khayyam Nightclub* in Yafo:

An imitation of life.

How lovely it would be
To share these things with her —
Haifa and the blue Mediterranean,
Ein Karem,
The sisters and the priests,
Jaffa and the soft breezes, the
few palm trees.

I lost her to another —
She did not desert me.
  She was coming.
I could have her now.
    But then
I did not understand —
  So I go on.

I have seen the way men live.

Jerusalem is only in the keeping of
        the Arabs.
They do not live in it. It is empty.
They are only its custodians.
Its high places have been brought low —
Until such time as we enter.
From that moment it shall be called,
"*Beulah, Faithful City — City of Right-
        eousness*";
And Righteousness shall be its seat,
Righteousness shall be its footstool —
The presentday "New City" is not this.

Some white birds
And the sun
Coming out.

Love them that hate you.

Domus Sancti Jacob (Saint Jacob Hostel)

So what if there is no food one night,
So what if there is no food two nights,
So what if there is no food three nights.

On seeing a photo of Adolph Eichmann
in the press:

"Do good unto them that
Do evil unto you" — why not?
Eichmann, he has done evil unto you.
Free him. Do good unto him —
He cannot pay for these crimes.

On thinking of my
parents with love:
I do not need them.

When they come dirty, clean them,
When they are hungry, feed them,
When they are Eichmann, free them.
When they come naked, clothe them,
When they come tired, put them to sleep.
Verily it has been said, "An eye for an
eye and a tooth for a tooth,"
But I say unto you, "When they hit thee
On the one cheek, turn the other cheek.
Do good unto them that do evil unto
you."

On the bus from Tel Aviv to Haifa
when the news of Eichmann's
sentence is announced:

They do not care,
They have become numb,
There is no reaction.
I see one woman —
Is she crying or
Is she sleeping?
She is sleeping.

Look at the oranges —
Too soon.
It comes
later.

Stella Maris: Star of the Sea

By the side of
The Mediterranean
I shall find my peace.

I do not marry
A girl
I do not love.

"*Stella Maris*" —
"Star of the Sea" —
I live here.

On seeing a woman who
did not control well:

I am a woman.
The control of this
piece of
The world is mine.
My spirit controls
This body. In it
is me,
I direct the way of
its coming,
The way of its motion,
The way of its giving
motion.
This is me.
It is not my name,
My home, my country.

On thinking of last year
in Paris and Persia:

You must live every day.
Like food — you must eat.
What was wrong then is
still wrong now.
When your time comes,
You will be chosen.

Had you just waited,
She would have come.

The moment never came.
It can come now.
People do not always
Come at the same time.

It comes like a flash —
It was in all
The things I did:
My trip to the West —
She, what was so uncertain,
Her times at school,
That moment in Paris,
Her going home.

There was the moment in Paris
When you were as I loved you.
I should not have lost you —
Neither should your life be a ruin.
Do you remember how you were
in Paris,
That one moment away from home,
strong —
And sometimes at school? This is
how
I want you. You have nothing to
fear.

I felt I was lost,
But with one stroke I broke it
And got on the right way.

On Being Lost

It is like
Swimming in a storm
And being hit by waves.
If one keeps on,
One will get there.

It's like coming to a station
And getting on a train
And going perpendicular
To the way you want to go.
You can either keep on going
On the wrong way
Or get off the moving train.
Go to the right
Which is already going on.
It is possible —
It takes courage.
One must strike off
Through much undergrowth
And much forest.
But, if you want to,
In one stroke you can do it —
The undergrowth is inside.

Come to me then.
Come to me lean,
Come to me as I
Once I knew thee,
No cigarettes —
strong.

The mind cannot see
Or thinks it can,
But sees only for the moment.
The other is one's intuition.
It is always better
To rely on that.
Better not to do what
The mind thinks it sees,
But what one feels.
When there is no light inside,
A man becomes brute-like.
He steps, he trudges,
His life becomes drudgery.

A man's spirit is like a canvas.
We paint upon it colors.
The colors depend on where he is.
We can change the colors,
Not what came before the colors.
The way of its spirit is his, despite
the colors.
His country has no bearing. It is
simply color.

I feed on the sky,
The sunsets
And sunrises —
And on the sea.

One night to get wet,
One night no sleep,
I don't care.

An anchor here,
An anchor there —
        a job.
A fight here,
A fight there.
I don't care. I am
        free.

Robert Eisenman is a man.
He is whole no matter where —
No matter under what conditions.

The charm of life has returned,
Like soft odours and sweet wine.

This book is like sweet wine.

A pink sea!

On Entering the German Sister's Convent
in Haifa

On the last sixteen days:

Is it only two weeks?
No wonder they were surprised.
To them, it is nothing;
To me, a lifetime.
Before this is infinite time —
When a man lets go,
Time is everywhere.

On the German sister:

There she was crying
Over the things that
They lost in the war.
O Lord, wasn't that
just too bad?

This is the beginning
Of my twenty-fifth year.
Now I can see out beyond.

The night,
The children singing —
Arab songs —
The white sky, the bells.

On the German sisters:

I do not approve of my sisters
Being other men's servants,
Especially not for money.

Forgive them Father,
If they serve You,
At least their eyes are blind
In the right direction
If they are blind,
They are locked on You.

On meeting a Polish Jew who came from Chinese Manchuria with his Children:

So, therefore, the Jews came as strangers. People do not like strangers.
Besides they, supposedly, had killed their god.
All men remember their own, even the stranger. They were twenty to a hundred.
In America all men are strangers, therefore the Jew is not special.
The history is the thing — all men are a part.
There is one thing there, Christians and Jews. However, there are others too,
So for all the world, how men got somewhere,
The "how" is the thing — not the present.
Knowing how, one fashions what is to come. Time is the potter's clay.
All men are under the control of what happened before.

On the Bible
(while reading Jeremiah):

This is higher than mathematics
For mathematics does not
Teach a man how to live —
This is the forgotten art.

On meeting an old man come from
Vienna and Boston:

Let him be at peace.
He has come home.
He sees the end of his time.
However, show him what
is to come —
He sees his time
But the whole of time,
Let him see for a moment.

"Your sins are forgiven you"

A sin is a mistake, an act committed out of
Temporary blindness, a momentary weakness.
"Your sins arm forgiven you" as certainly
As you wake up in the morning and there is
a new day.
Who among you has not sinned?
Who among you has not forgotten
The eternal purpose of things?

I have not to refuse
That which is given to me
In times of plenty.
There will be plenty
Of lean times, about
Which to complain.

Your future?
It is for Tel Aviv.
What are you holding back for?

Holding on? Let yourself go.
Be at peace, become great,
become strong:
Your heart, it is Jesus,
Your love, it is the world,
Your spirit, it is the poet's,
Your people, you are a Jew;
Your country, it is America —
Hold on to none of them.

PART FIVE

THE SOUL OF TEL AVIV

1961–62

On Looking for a Room

You can pull things just so much.
There is a way, some tension —
Then it breaks.

There is nothing you cannot do.
It is all in the way you do it.

I will face the things
Which they have faced
And come out higher.
There is nothing you
cannot face.

The Highest Way is the sky.
There is nothing but blue.

You have
To have
Courage —
Always.

Now you follow colors —
The blue is here.

You must be firm.
There is only one way.
That is the Lord.
There are not two.

I have found a way to live —
This is not a profession.
It is a religion.

Teach it to your children — rules
to follow.
Then they will not have to
Undergo what you have undergone.
Each man does this
Which is why nations, customs,
wars —
But you must do it higher.

Life is not as simple as I thought.
My family, my home, my environment? Yes.
But how to live, what is possible, the
Highest Way? No.

He
Seeks the
Highest Way.

How I settled down:

Something inside me
Makes the decision for me
Without my knowing it.

She:

It was done when you came up from Greece
And gave her the precious signet stone.
Better to have left it then
And gone on to Italy — don't bring back
corpses.

When society does not give a woman an outlet,
When there is nothing to look beautiful for,
She does not look beautiful — e.g., France.

A Teacher

A teacher teaches men how to live:
Aristotle, Socrates, Jesus.
Today we teach subjects
Descended from their schools.
We teach men how to be parts — not
the whole.

On going into the city:

There is nothing which frightens me more.
It is like a soldier giving up his armor.
There is nothing *outside* which frightens me.

On Sitting on Dizengoff Street:

This is no more serious
Than
Sitting
In East Orange, New Jersey.

Teaching:

It is not for me
To teach their children.
It is for me to teach *them*.

The Spirit of the Room

They do not believe
Any longer in
Evil spirits,
Because they have
Forgotten
What the men
Who saw them knew.

Ode to a Used Prophylactic on
the Beach in Tel Aviv

O thou enchanted symbol of
Our mechanical civilization,
O thou pot of *tsouris,*
O thou rusted remnant of
Man's uncompleted fornication.
To see you here,
Have you followed me this far —
Even here, along the Lord's holy
beaches?

This is the root,
The source of all things.
One sees here how things began.

On Receiving a Letter from the Draft
Board:

I do not believe in nations,
I do not believe in countries,
I do not believe there is room
Any longer for them in the world.
Because I was born in one place
Makes me no different than a man
born in another.
I shall not kill him, I will not fight,
I shall not serve.

I set out at twenty-one to find —
Fame, fortune, honour, history?
I know not what. And I found?
I know not what.

Notes while Reading the Penguin *Hinduism*

The loss of self is a natural want,
An identification with everything,
A loss of desires, a return to the
great stream
Where even death has no effect, but
a passage —
A jolt when the body is rigid, full
of pride,
Non-existent when the self no more
exists.

So we say these men believe
Because certain men came along
And saw the world in a certain way,
Because the Hindus came along
And saw similar spirits in animals
and men.

Of course, the Hindus have it —
Jesus is a divine incarnation.
Nothing other than God exists.
The universe is His manifestation.
God may have multiple human incarnations,
Avatars:
Rama, Krishna, Buddha — Buddhism.
The concepts are related.
History has taken different paths in
different places.
You see "Jesus" is nothing but Buddha,
Is nothing but Perfection —
An incarnation of the Divine.

Christianity and Judaism are the same thing.
Now that the Jews have come back to their
own Land,
They shall be combined.
They will then become Hinduism.
The Lord is *Brahman,* Jesus is *Atman.*
Combine the two — you have Hinduism.

When the Jews and Christians are reunited,
Then shall the world be ready
For its four corners to come together.
History takes its time with different peoples
in different ways —
Different events and different colors,
And all remembered. New things shall be
remembered
And their memories joined to the Truth.

I am on the path of Truth.
There is no Truth without
happiness.
Truth is joy. It is the power
to
Change one's environment
and bring happiness.

If, as the scientists have
discovered,
Matter is not matter at all
But energy or waves,
Could it not be that
What look to us like forms
Are not forms at all,
What look to us like people
Are not people at all,
What look to us like desires:
Anger, fear, misery, unhappiness —
Are not desires at all,
But all representations
Of imperfect states of being?
Could such an impossibility be?
And death too and life —
Just states of becoming
As the Hindus seem to think?
Could it not be that
This earth is the Hell —
The Inferno of Dante?
And Heaven, "The Kingdom of
God" — the becoming,
The steps into the Highness,
the world beyond.

Father Jacques and
Hinduism

When the flesh
Becomes the word,
Then is it the soul —
The soul, the Lord;
The three become one.
In Hinduism God is
worshipped
In different forms.
So too with "Jesus" —
An incarnation of
Godliness,
"The King of the
Jews," etc.

You see why the Christians think "Jesus" God? He is.
You see what the Buddhists call an incarnation of
the Divine?
You see what the Jews have never seen — being blind
and chosen?
He, who is blinded by his representation in history;
Chosen, so as to become blinded by his chosenness;
the history — the becoming.

The Jews are enslaved — there is no doubt of that —
By their history and their bodies, by the events of
time,
For they never received redemption, salvation,
resurrection —
(After Father Jacques) the things they were building for.
O you Chosen of God, free yourselves if He is your God.
Then He is not just your God and you are but an
historical representation.

I will tell you why I like wandering so much.
Because life itself is a journey
And no matter how permanent it may seem,
It has its deaths and entrances —
Everything you build is blown away.

But this is not the whole of it.
It is more in keeping with
The Higher Way of life,
To come to a place, work,
And not become involved in
The contortions of being set up —
You are already set up.
I think this is why in the end
I went out from America,
Because I could not see where
All that effort was leading —
And all those day-to-day perturbations.

One may perfect
These things
Like everything.

God
Is the
Perfect spirit.

If I knew then
What I know now,
But I learned now
What I knew then.

We teach subjects,
But not control over one's self.
One needs entirely different things
To settle down.

1962, Yoo hoo!

Nineteen Hundred and Sixty-two

A black man told me last night,
"Did you see the lightning?"
It rained all night
On the darkened streets
And the rain fell down in droves.
The ships on the Mediterranean
Blew their horns in the night.
What was there so nice in
The sound of those words?
Of course, two black Africans —
Two Angels beckoning to me.

On the New Year:

The signposts are all gone.
I shall follow it wherever it goes:
New plans, new shores, new loves — perhaps.

I was lost in
The forest of the people.
Now is there light.

The Palestinian boys?
Of course, what they had,
The English honour —
The Jewish soul and the Christian
code.
That is why they won then and
not now.
Now there will be only disaster.
I want to get out
Before the sky falls in
And the bottom falls out.

You see it is not
To be perfected here.
Work is the way to
Carve it in blood.

The way —
It is so
Delicate.

As long
As I am in the city,
I want company — people to love.

On the Mad Prophet I Met:

Perhaps he is right.
Tel Aviv is the center —
The lost Jerusalem.

Across the Street from the Restaurant

Do you not see how
The Lord blesses you if you but look?
In the center of the city on a tree —
A bird hanging upside down on flower buds.

Tel Aviv

Dialogue in the City
with Self:

You are a sloppy fellow,
Prone to appetites,
They would say —
Your nails, your room,
Your bed, your eating.
It is a wonder your spirit
comes out.

The soul is a mirror.
One takes one's image
From the world it reflects.
One becomes Tel Aviv
Or Sasa, or Paris or India,
Or one's work or one's love.
When one does nothing,
One keeps looking in
The mirror at one's self.

Types:

This is why
I am on this earth —
To inhabit this beautiful frame.

On a Rooftop in Tel Aviv

Have you ever shaved
On a rooftop at night
By the light of the moon?
I have — in Tel Aviv.

On seeing a boy and a girl
holding hands over the
table:

How many girls' hands
Have you held like that?
My God none — only one.

And you say, you do not
love her?
No, I do not love her.
You lie. I don't. You do.
This is ridiculous,
Said Alice to wonderland.

And so it is goodbye,
So time has passed us by,
So a moment has come,
And then been lost —
No more for you and I.

And so it is goodbye,
So fond hopes too must die,
So dreams and love must pass away,
And memories take their place —
So memories too shall die.

And so it is goodbye,
So life must take us on —
Two streams once united now
diverging,
No way to change their course,
No way to stop their flood.

A life was lived and lived
passed on,
So dreams shall fade away.

On smelling
the night air
in Tel Aviv:

The word is
Still with me.
It gives me strength.

On looking at the people
of the world:

O Lord, is this not why
We are on the earth,
To master ourselves?

So for the moment
You inhabit that grey suit —
Are you so proud?
Or so blind?

This book is power,
This book is strength.

One should not worry
About money spent,
Money not spent.
Follow the way,
Follow the cool breezes.

I shall throw
Money away
For this thing.
I shall throw
Everything away
For this thing.

In the Cafe

We are all on this earth together.
This does not mean
We should forget ourselves
By talking meaningless nonsense
To each other.
This explains it.
We are all sitting here talking,
Seeking something
From each other, from women —
Our modes, our acts, our attitudes.
This explains the high and the low.
Your feet are on the ground;
Your sex organs, a hole;
But your head, your spirit,
Hold it high, let it rise.
Do not be distracted,
Captured, trapped in
The tunnels of the city, its subways.
They exist no more than passing
From New York to San Francisco
Via Chicago or Des Moines —
They are not necessary.
Let your spirit rise —
From birth, from death,
From children, from desires.
As the Indians say,
Release yourself
From the eternal cycle.

Do things
With a very
Delicate touch.

You are here on this earth.
Consider it a stage.
You can either mock the fact
That you are here
Or elevate it.
I believe in this last —
Every day, every moment.

Do not hesitate,
Make a decision and then go on.
Hesitation is corrosive.
Later you can change it.

Never go back.
Always go on.
Go back only
In going on.

Your food, your environment,
Your surroundings
Are the food you eat —
You imbibe upon them.

Whatever the problem,
The whole thing is this,
To take it in stride
And move over it as it comes
With daring, softness, and
finesse.
For whatever happens
On the way will come
And you must somehow pass
by —
Therefore, pass by well.

Standing in the railroad-bus
terminal in Haifa:

So this is where it
Has led me after two years.
You were not so intelligent then.
There was a good deal
You did not then know.

"Go on, go on!"
My soul cries out.
I went so far
There was no place
left to go,
Yet still I want to
be going.

It is no more lovely to see
A man make a mockery of his life
Than to see a dog grovel in the mud.

The seeds were sown,
Yet they blow away
In the wind.

The choice was made which covers
All choices you make now —
Except how well you live.

"The Way" —
To what?
"The Way to
Perfection."

On seeing a girl walk by with noble
bearing:

She does not see
That the nicest thing is
The way the wind touches her hair.

They want me to settle myself,
To make a nest to seduce women.
Is this what I live for — never!

You have to go slowly,
You cannot think of home.
Though you love your father and mother,
You cannot go home now
But pray it will be still there
In three to four more years —
Please, Lord, keep it there for me.

To any woman,
Make one advance,
One motion,
Then end it.
Otherwise it becomes
A necessity —
Your rotten pride.

The trail through "the Way"
Is like the part in
One's hair.

The world is but a stage
And we, all the actors upon it.
Each man has his part to play,;
His life — his entrances.

On sitting in the cafe and
seeing the people:

And so the world walks by,
Generation after generation.
It is time for you to play
Your role upon its stage.

Of course man is suspicious.
The point is to cover over your wants with
such power
As to make them enjoyable for the other.
For yourself, the victory is enjoyment
enough.

Never let down,
Never with the people,
Never with your family,
Never with your love —
Perhaps with God.

Regard *Bon Dieu* How I Free Myself

My father's business —
Why must I support myself?
To hold myself up —
From life, from death?
They are the same.
I need not to
Devote myself to this.
Then what to do with
The rest of my life —
Seduce women with my ears,
Clear myself of fears?
Why fear? Of pain,
Of ignorance, of suffering?
When the spirit is free,
How great and wise —
What a noble and
Marvelous universe.
Am I incarnated
And this poor flesh weak?
How it wanders while my eyes
And spirit soar. And my mind —
The balance between the two.
Do I cling to this poor flesh?
Forgive me —
How noble to combine.

I don't live to work,
To keep myself alive,
To own marvelous things.
No, I'm sorry if I
Disappoint you, father.
Perhaps you are not, then,
my father.

I love you Mediterranean

You are not
So nice from here Mediterranean.
But still, knowing what you are, I love you.

On the loosing of the birds that
were about to be killed:

By whose authority
Do you do this?
By my Father's authority.

There is a game played at bars.
One has to know the rules
If you want to win.

This is
The sewer
Of the world.

To Nueves

How beautiful you are
tonight.
Just to see you move or
See your mouth once in
a day
Twist into smile, or your
eyes —
How beautiful you are
tonight.

An Affair of Honour

Nor was I lacking
The courage, or the words.
Nor was there fear or uncertainty.
The only thing lacking was the will.

It is the joy of action —
Like being in the saddle.
No wonder people like Westerns.

Thoughts at the Cafe Kasit:

In order to give up woman
A man has got to give
Up everything.

On thinking of my cousin:

You see, Lord, the fate
You almost led me into?

On Art

It is the mode or fashion
Now to look up to,
In some circles even to adore,
The artist who perfects things.
How much higher it is
To perfect one's spirit.
The artist works with things
We can touch or see —

The products of one's spirit.
His work day upon day,
Month after month,
Brings with it its reward,
The perfection he seeks.
But what of the artist himself —
What kind of man is he?
This we neglect, not only to ask,
But even to look or see.
The artist gets his reward
If he succeeds.
But what rewards are there
For the man who seeks
Perfection in his spirit?
Of this, we cannot speak.
There is an element
In each artist's labor —
Each writer, each painter,
Of fortune seeking.
He gets his recompense —
Fame and renown, if he succeeds.
But how much more difficult is it
To pursue perfection within oneself.
Where is the commission for this,
Where is the renown —
One does not know.
The artist works with things seen:
Paints, clay, words, and the like.
But what is the stuff of
The artist of the spirit?
It is the soul.
How much finer the rewards
To work with such stuff
Than to work with any of these others.
Yet how much more precarious,
How many thousand times
More the danger of failure.
These were the early "Christians" —
They were artists of the soul.

I have turned the corner.
The flood's been stopped.

I change,
But the word does not change.
The word will stop
This rotting away of the flesh.

A Poem to Nueves on the Night She would not Dance

The night tonight is very lovely —
So too then the halved moon.
You would not see me, it is true,
But so too, then, you would not
dance for him.
This is the thing I like in you.

The California Cafe

I have not written a poem
To a girl in a long time.
She touches something within me.
For me, there is nothing else
in this cafe.

Each is an action that
Changes in some way the world.
When you do nothing, nothing
happens.

Myself is a nice,
Soft character who
Doesn't want any trouble.

Be a ghost —
Next month you
Will be twenty-five.

On challenging him
to fight:

I have no stomach
for it.

This is the meaning of
Your stay here —
You want to dance
Upon the stage of life.

The next day comes and
Continues on to this one —
I begin to feel it come back.

Either a man is held up by nothing
Or he settles himself on rock
Which is well-formed —
In which case
His spirit is held up by the Lord.

Neither
Do I shirk
From it.

The End of January, 1962

Now I understand it.
The problem is right action.
It is to do, to act.
Uncertainty is debilitating.
A man pays in modern terms
For his hesitation in money.
It is for this a man
Does not have to act.
It is this one sees
In the faces of the shopkeepers,
The merchants, the rich,
Their faces sunk in decrepitude —
The sinking of the spirit.
It is for this a man takes
Such pride in his clothes —
The cowboy, the bullfighter.
The clothes are a sign of right
Action once performed well —
see their faces.

I understand now
Libations and sacrifices —
They drove away the evil spirits,
There was certainty for action.
It is not in woman.

An Open Letter to the
Jewish People:

I have heard cries.
You are eating each other up —
A meal more than Paris,
A room more than London.
You are not in Europe,
You cannot go on raising
the prices.
For what, your blindness?
To own a car, a motorcycle,
To sit in the cafe with a
new suit?
No, it is not right.
This is a wonderful land,
This is what the Bible is
all about —
What was written then.
I do not want to see you
All driven into the sea.
You must rise above being
"Jews."
Shopkeeper must not gobble
up shopkeeper.

Why were we born so imperfect?
Tell me, why were we born if
We are not prepared for the journey?
I want to know.
Where is the force necessary
To live correctly?
It must be in me somewhere.

Every action is
Not so important.
Do not press it
Into significance.

There was no charm.

The father looked back in time.
One son looked forward —
Who knows why?
They both now come together.

On getting into a fight
in Tel Aviv:

I feel better now.
My action there was
Better than my hesitation.
It is this a woman
Senses like an animal —
This Hemingway writes
about.

And where does "Christ"
Fit into all of this?
He is the perfection,
He walks upon the waters.
He is above them all
Looking down from
The heights of Heaven
(Nirvana).

I have a
New vocabulary.
It is like learning Greek.

I have solved
The problem of
Right action.

I see now
The Highness
Of the Greek way.

Poetry is the
Righteousness
Of the spirit.

"You are a cosmopolitan," he said.
Of course, that is what you
Are trying to do.

You see why women enjoy a fighter?
Who is the second — you see it follows —
The man with money.
Money takes the place of right action.
It is why "buying" is such a dirty word.

You see now what your fear brought you
Even at the age of ten —
Bad eyesight, fatness.
You shied away from things.
Father, why did you not help me then?
You see, you should have
Continued playing football
And not listened to your mind.
You would have grown strong.
And even now, your sentimentality,
Your smiles, are debilitating.
They hold you back.
Once you have decided against a thing,
Do not go back to that thing.
If only it could have been so with her.
You should have gone on to Paris in mid-winter.
This way you lost a year.
Perhaps you will never go now to India.
Your destiny is catching up to you.
This is your twenty-fifth year
And your father needs you —
Perhaps you have forfeited it.

No wonder there was such joy
In seeing us act when I was young —
And the fathers going to the football games
To see their sons *act well*
(I can go to India another time).

No wonder the Lord weakened your sight.
You deserved it, cowardly one.
No wonder the ancient peoples,
Who knew more about this life than we,
Identified the testicles with the sight.

Wills studied in order
To achieve his perfection.
It took years in Paris.
It softened and changed him.
His parents died,
He let go of everything —
For the word, the charm,
the gesture
(I saw a moment's slip).
However it is a perfection
of the soul.
He did not give up architecture
for nothing.

One should step back a moment or
up Higher,
One should choose one's words.
One should perfect one's soul
In this world, not the next —
For success, for woman,
For honour? I know not.

By choosing your words very
precisely,
So as to express your thoughts
honestly,
You can get through any crisis.

I know now the highest obligation of life.
It was never even mentioned.
Theirs was only to eat, to sleep, to work,
But there is something Higher,
For every man will do these.
It is the way it is done —
In anger, in pride,
To thieve, to rob, to lie, to crawl.
The end is nothing without the way.
Otherwise, men will hack though
To what they want like dumb brutes.
The door opens in the end
Only to the soft and loving touch.

You see there are numerous doors —
Some open until one does not.
For the man who walks upon the waters,
Every door will open,
Every knee give way,
Every tongue give praise.

Every road
Comes to him
Who walked best.

Do you know why I don't like life in America?
Because life there only goes up to a certain
point and then stops,
People only grow up to a certain point and then stop.
The standard planted at the middle of society
for one to strive towards
Is democracy and freedom. This is the religion,
But there is no standard of excellence, no standard
of "Jesus Christ,"
Nothing for one to elevate one's self for.

You see now
Why he could walk on water?
You see why "the Devil"
Could not stand before him?
You see how a man blessed
Could do these things?

See what you have forgotten, democracies?
Bend down you nations in your pride.
Make way, make way, for the Son of Man.
O Heavens, sing loud songs and every soul
jump — rejoicing,
For he comes on soft tiptoes and the whole
earth gives way.

There were moments offered me —
Doors to enter:
The university, physics,
Doctor, professor,
Passage to Singapore,
Post in Aix-en-Provence —
I followed some Higher Way.

Why then I saw nothing,
        I know not.
Now there are four times
Twenty-five years' work
        to be done.

When there is
No money left,
There is yourself.

The word is in me and fills me up.
I will make my flesh
The instrument of this word.

I will tell you what is missing in this Land.
What is missing is nobility,
What is missing is grace,
What is missing is "Jesus Christ" (Honour).

I am a cup,
I am a vessel,
With one thought,
One idea —
"Jesus Christ."

All these emotions
In everyday life
Become perfected,
Refined, extended.

You see this all comes with "Jesus."
You say he has no place in the Twentieth Century?
More now than any other.
How to resolve a poem about a milk machine?
With a trip to the Holy Land — "Jesus."

This is how I did my growing up.

I could have ridden in the hills of the Upper Galilee,
I could have been a doctor, physicist, lawyer,
I could have worked my way to Singapore,
I could have taught in Aix-en-Provence —
I chose to do none of these things.
I chose to do something Higher.

With my traveling
I have confused the fates,
I have clouded the necessities.

If a man is the sum total
Of his choices,
Then I am nothing.

What has caused this?
You see,
All the things you could not do,
You found are possible to be done —
And still you wake up again the next day.

Above: Author sitting in front of the Acropolis, January, 1959, looking innocent and suitably serious. European friends still say — a la Al Gore and the internet — that he was the first to introduce wearing white tennis shoes on a daily basis into Europe (his traditional college white bucks having worn out). *N.b.*, the empty stillness of the Acropolis at that time — still devoid of the waves of tourists that came with the later overrflow of jet transport.

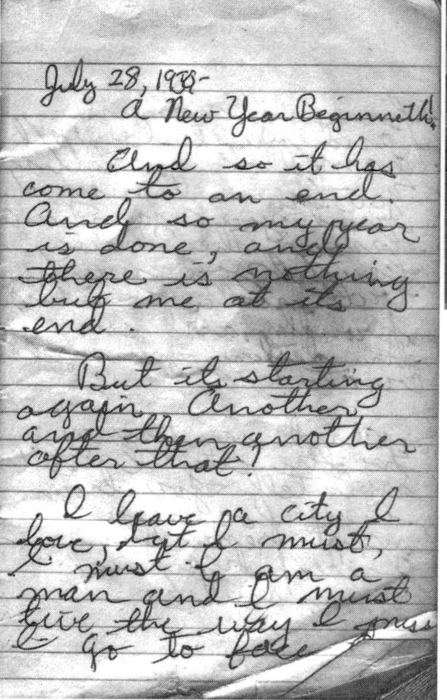

July 28, 195[illegible]-
A New Year Beginneth!
And so it has come to an end. And so my year is done, and there is nothing but me at its end.
But its starting again. Another and then another after that!
I leave a city I love, but I must, I must. I am a man and I must live the way I must
Go to face

Above: The Rue de l'Odeon looking down toward the Carrefour de l'Odeon and the Monaco Cafe: "And this is what Paris has meant to me...that a man can survive...This is Paris, the microcosm of our universe — all things concentrated there, all things magnified there" (see pp. 7-17, 70-80, etc.).

Left: The first entry into the Journal, leaving San Francisco, July 28, 1959, to hitchhike back across America (the author having already spent the previous year in Paris, Alt Aussee in Austria, Vienna, and Hydra in Greece) in five days and five nights before departing for Europe after spending some time on the North Beach scene (pp. 4-6).

LEFT: "And Heather, some sturdy emotion" (see p. 80) — "Do you remember Heather Seton? Do you remember what it was to be a woman?... A woman is in the the look, a woman is in the courage" (see p. 277). Heather walking on a Leicester Street, March, 1959, before going to Paris in May (also see pp. 82, 302-4, 321, etc.).

BELOW: Mme Rachou, the owner of "the Beat Hotel," standing in the doorway of 9 Rue Git-le-Coeur, where the author stayed from September, 1959-April, 1960 (Harold Chapman).

ABOVE: The Monaco Cafe, the main center of bohemian and artistic life on the Left Bank in Paris in the late Fifties and early Sixties (see pp. 71 and 79-80) before it disappeared into the presentday and now-chic "*Comptoir du Relais*"— author's wife and four children seated above at left in front of the Cafe some twenty-five years later.

ABOVE: Alex Campbell and John and Ian Bennetts playing outside the Monaco Cafe on the Carrefour de l'Odeon sometime in mid-1960 at the height of its influence (see pp. 71, 79-80, etc.). For John Bennetts, see also p. 256; for Alex Campbell, see p. 80 (Harold Chapman, *The Beat Hotel*, Paris, 1984).

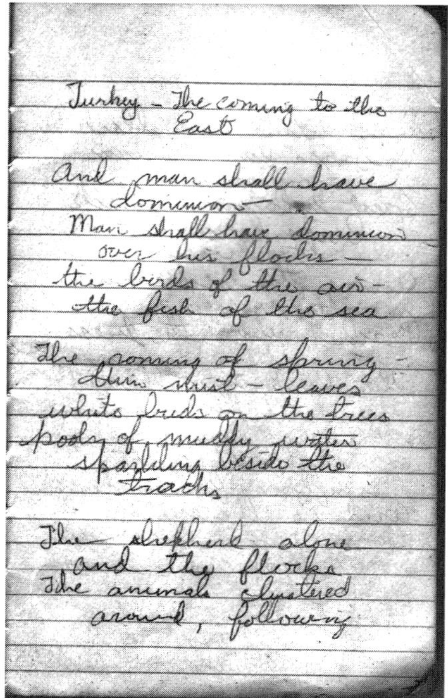

Turkey - The coming to the
East

And man shall have
dominion -
Man shall have dominion
over his flocks -
the birds of the air -
the fish of the sea

The coming of spring -
thin mist - leaves
white buds on the trees
pools of muddy water
sparkling beside the
tracks

The shepherd alone
and the flocks
The animals clustered
around, following

ABOVE MIDDLE: The location of "The Beat Hotel" at 9 Rue Git-le-Coeur near the Place St. Michel — the hotel is halfway down on the right with the Seine and the book stalls on the Quai de Grands Augustins just visible at end of street.

LEFT: First page of hand-written Diario — "*Part One: The Coming to the East*" (pp. 19-45): "And man shall have dominion. Man shall have dominion over his flocks -- the birds of the air, the fish of the sea."

RIGHT: Turkish student card from Istanbul, which enabled transit travelers to get low price transport on trains through Communist Yugoslavia, Bulgaria, or across Turkey further East.

№ 279

Adı : Robert
Soyadı : Eisenman
Tabiiyeti : A.B.D.
Üniversite : Stanford
Doğ. tarihi : 15-2-1937
Pass. No. : Z024493

RIGHT BELOW: Transit visa for Yugoslavia for use on the Orient Express. One bought the ticket in Vienna as far as Belgrade. There one got off the train while it waited for an hour in the station and, with one's black-market Yugoslav dinars (also bought in Vienna) and Turkish student card, ran in the cold (it was always cold in Yugoslav train stations) to buy a cheaper one for the rest of the way. The entire trip might have cost $20 (see pp. 20–23).

TRANZITNA — ~~DUPLA TRANZITNA~~
Transit simple — ~~Transit double~~
VIZA br. 03184
Važi za prolaz kroz FNR Jugoslaviju
Valable pour traverser la Yougoslavie
do / jusqu'au −5 AOUT 1961
Izdata / Délivré le −5 MAI 1961
Po ovlašćenju,

ABOVE LEFT: Barbara: "If only spirits could be summoned up" (see p. 26) and "Where more in time or space come oranges on the breeze?" (see p, 38; also see pp. 7-15, 62, 75, etc. — courtesy B. McNair).

There was the moon
full now
and venus and two
trees
And it had been right
It was trying to tell
me something

ABOVE LEFT: "There was the moon full now and Venus and two trees and I had been right. It had been trying to tell me something" (see p. 44).

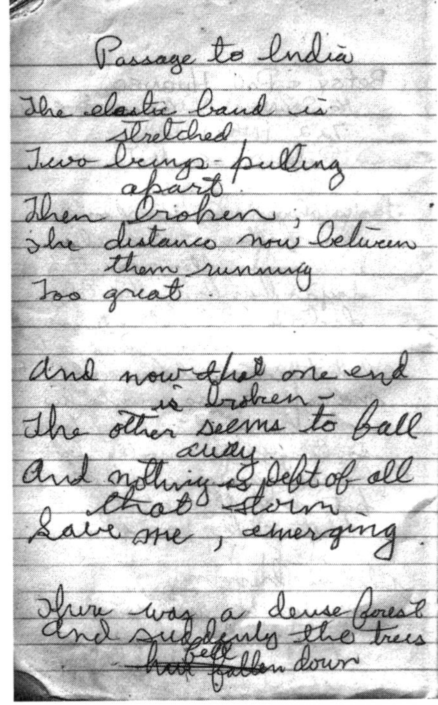

Passage to India
The elastic band is
stretched
Two beings pulling
apart
Then broken;
the distance now between
them running
Too great.

And now that one end
is broken
The other seems to fall
away
And nothing is left of all
that storm
Save me, emerging.

There was a dense forest
And suddenly the trees
~~had fallen~~ fell down

ABOVE RIGHT: Facing page in the Diario: "Passage to India — There was a dense forest and suddenly the trees fell down" (see p. 45).

Above: Author's friend Keith Lorenz paying Mme. Rachou for a cup of coffee in front of the Beat Hotel early Summer, 1960 (Harold Chapman).

Below: First Kennedy poem, greeting his nomination when disembarking from a Turkish ship in Piraeus, Greece, July 17th, 1960. This faces a page with a sketch of the island volcano of Stromboli, "the two lights of its jetty" visible from the deck of the boat (see pp. 49-50).

Above left: The Rue Git-le-Coeur looking up from the Seine towards Rue St. Andre des Arts, the Hotel at 9 Rue Git-le-Coeur half-way up the street on the left.

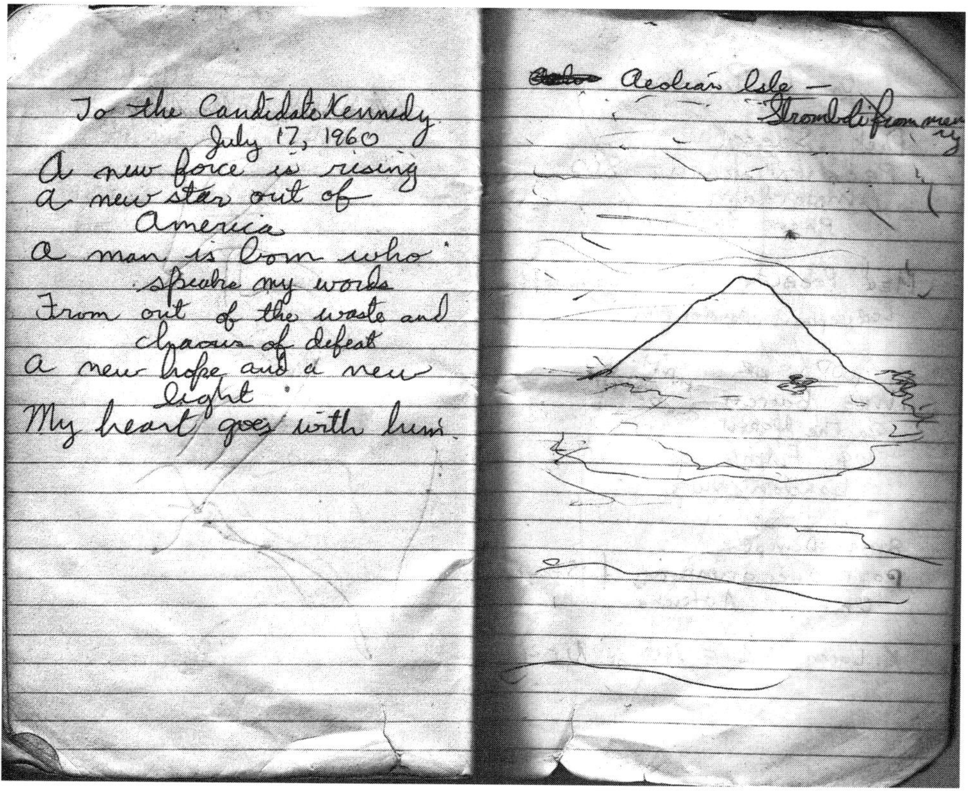

To the Candidate Kennedy
July 17, 1960
A new force is rising
a new star out of
America
a man is born who
speaks my words
From out of the waste and
chaous of defeat
a new hope and a new
light
My heart goes with him

Aeolian Isle —
Stromboli from

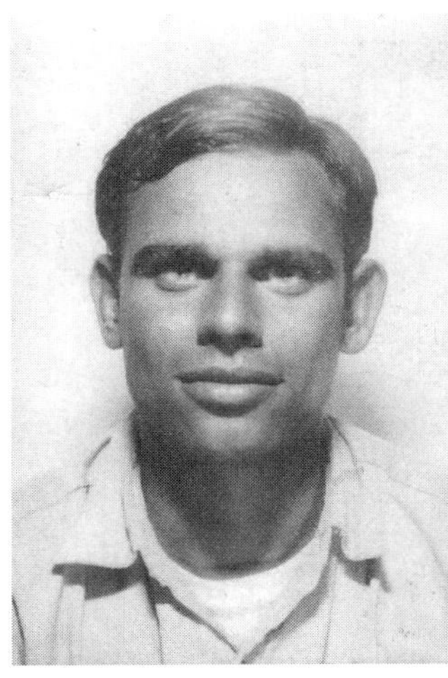

RIGHT: The archway cul-de-sac leading from Rue Git-le-Coeur and the end of Rue St. Andre des Arts to Place St. Michel.

LEFT: Paris Metro photobooth snapshot taken on author's return from Israel, July-August, 1960 — author looking very proud of his suntan-fit kibbutz-look (see pp. 52-60).

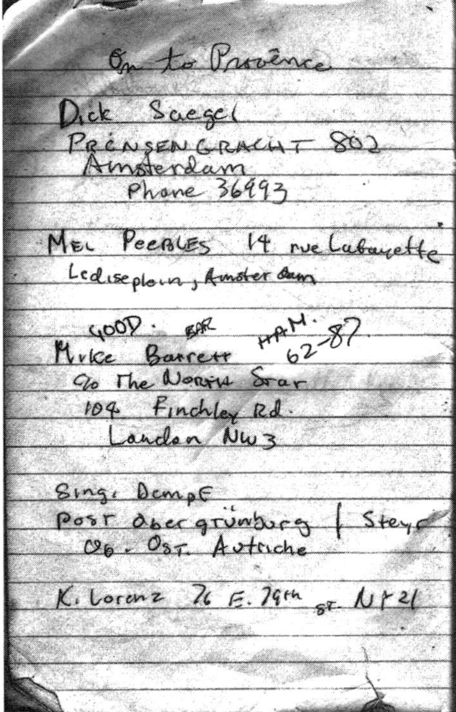

On to Provence

Dick Saegel
PRINSENGRACHT 802
Amsterdam
Phone 36993

MEL PEEBLES 14 rue Lubayette
Ledisepleim, Amsterdam

GOOD. BAR HAM. 62-87
Mike Barrett
c/o The North Star
104 Finchley Rd.
London NW3

Sing. Dempf
Post Obergrünburg | Steyr
Ob. Öst. Autriche

K. Lorenz 76 E. 79th St. NY21

ABOVE: Facing pages in Israel-Paris notebook, July-August, 1960. On the left: "On to Provence" with jottings referring to the author's best friends at the time: Keith Lorenz (see top left of preceding page) and Melvin Van Peebles (also see p. 256 mentioning John Bennetts, etc.) — on the right "Heather in the Mirror," drawn in a room in the Grand Hotel des Balcons, Rue Casimir Delavigne, August, 1960.

U.S. MERCHANT MARINER'S DOCUMENT
ISSUED BY
UNITED STATES COAST GUARD

NAME
Robert "H" EISENMAN

Z OR BK NUMBER	DATE OF BIRTH
Z-1168800	2-15-37

PLACE OF BIRTH	CITIZENSHIP
New Jersey	USA

HOME ADDRESS
4 Washington Square
New York, N.Y.

Robert H. Eisenman
SIGNATURE OF MARINER

TOP LEFT: Highly-prized Seaman's card, showing Washington Square Village address (see, p. 61), which author was able to get at Seaman's Hall because a friendly tugboat captain took pity on him. It was never ultimately used, but always highly prized (see p. 62 below: "Tonight are all the ships gone out to sea. I think it's time to part").

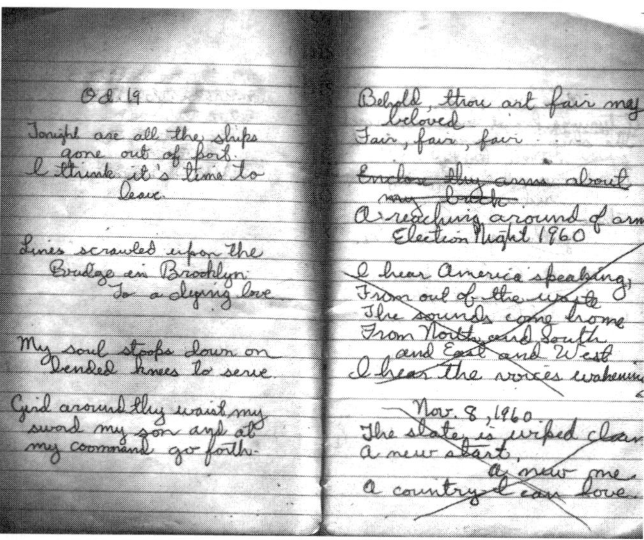

Oct 19

Tonight are all the ships
gone out of port.
I think it's time to
leave.

Lines scrawled upon the
Bridge in Brooklyn
To a dying love

My soul stoops down on
bended knees to serve.

Gird around thy waist my
sword my son and at
my command go forth.

Behold, thou art fair my
beloved
Fair, fair, fair

~~Enclose thy arms about~~
~~my back~~
A reaching around of arm
Election Night 1960

I hear America speaking,
From out of the waste
The sounds come frome
From North and South
and East and West
I hear the voices wakenin

Nov. 8, 1960.
The slate is wiped clean
a new start,
a new me.
a country I can love.

LEFT: Facing pages in the Diario from October 19th and November 8th, Election Night 1960, the next Kennedy allusions. The poems are crossed out because of author's later disillusionment over the Patrice Lumumba assassination in the Congo, the Bay of Pigs, and subsequent Vietnam irresponsibilities. The Oct. 19th lines: "To a dying Love" relate to thinking of departure and trying to "ship out" as above (see pp. 62-73) and the poem at the top of the facing page: "Behold thou art fair, my beloved, fair, fair, fair," shows that the author was continuing to read the Bible, which he had begun the previous spring in his room in "the Beat Hotel" in Paris and continued on the kibbutz in Israel ("Kibbutz Sasa" — see pp. 24-33).

President Kennedy, I salute
you sir.
With you there ushers in
a new era
With you has come the
flowering age.
Perhaps you shall not live
to see it done,
Who knows, perhaps not
even its fruition,
But you have ridden on
its tide
And though the balance was
uncertain,
Though its conception was
precarious,
The thing is done, a direction
is set,
Not now to be undone.

And I shall be the
chronicler of that age.

The spirit which came
down to me,
From my father before me
and his fathers.
That spirit that grew
undamaged, though
battered,
Battered by my mother's
~~clan~~ race
A clan of monetary men,
though meaning well
Of fear and inhibition,
of slavery
(That short success so
pitifully claimed)
That spirit of the wandering
Jew,
The wanderer, my

BOTTOM LEFT: The greetings to Kennedy continue — now as "President Kennedy" (see pp. 64-7), since the election has been completed; but there is also a possible prophetic note should one choose to regard it.

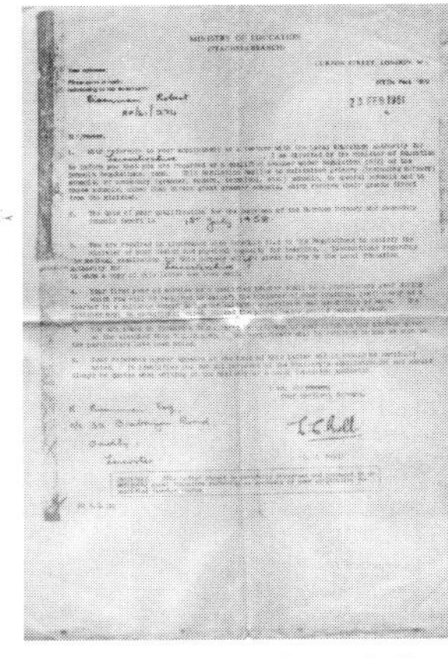

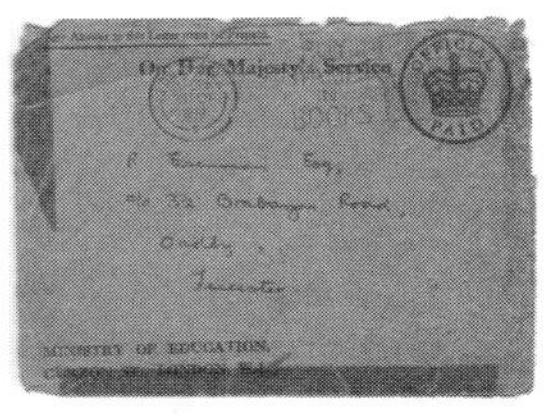

LEFT: United Kingdom Ministry of Education Permit with envelope mailed to Leicestershire address, dated February 23rd, 1961 certifying author as a reserve secondary school teacher (see pp. 82-85: "Leicestershire in Winter").

BELOW LEFT: "Heather Seton — You are my sister that was not born and I am your brother that was not born," February, 1961 (see p. 82 above).

BELOW: Heather Seton Poem entry in the journals following the line: "Another moon and night" (also see the later "Venus kept leaving her hair for me," p. 321, and "You are my Zipporah," p. 302).

ABOVE LEFT: The author's brother, the well-known future architect Peter Eisenman ("Do well, my brother. Build mighty buildings. One day we shall put them to some use" — see p. 437; also pp. 155, 161, 171, 441-445), standing with Heather in back garden, January, 1961, author just visible upper right.

Another moon and
night.

Heather Seton

You are my sis-
ter that was-
n't born
And I am your
brother that
was not
born.

Hold up your head
high my girl
There is blood
between us.

Aprodite

Do you smile on me
tonight Venus,
The one bright star
in all the sky.
Are you beside me
once again, oh
Venus
Do you hear the chil-
dren playing?
You in the clear and
February sky
descending;
Are you the same?
The one the Greeks
called Aprodite.

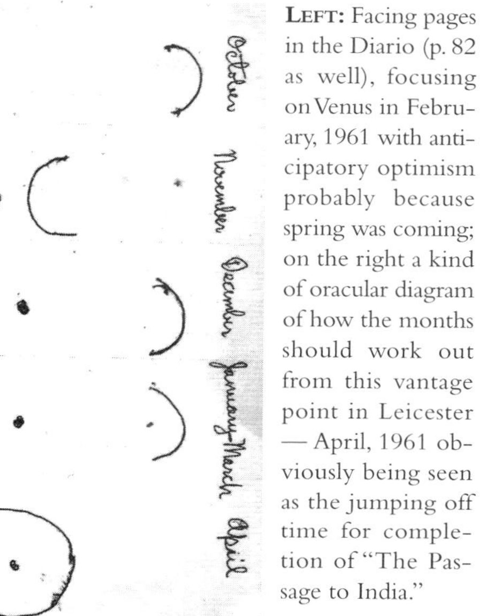

LEFT: Facing pages in the Diario (p. 82 as well), focusing on Venus in February, 1961 with anticipatory optimism probably because spring was coming; on the right a kind of oracular diagram of how the months should work out from this vantage point in Leicester — April, 1961 obviously being seen as the jumping off time for completion of "The Passage to India."

ABOVE LEFT: Strange song in the notebooks celebrating "Kennedy's Inauguration Day," exuding optimism and written at the end of January, 1961, obviously before the assassination of Lumumba, the Bay of Pigs, etc.

ABOVE RIGHT: As the poem on the facing page opposite continues, it reads: "Hold up your head high, my girl. There is blood between us" — see as well the later pensive note on p. 304: "Yes my dear Heather, I have many children now. The Children of Israel are all my children."

ABOVE LEFT: John Seton. See poem "To Mr. Seton" right from the notebooks facing the future-months' diagram..

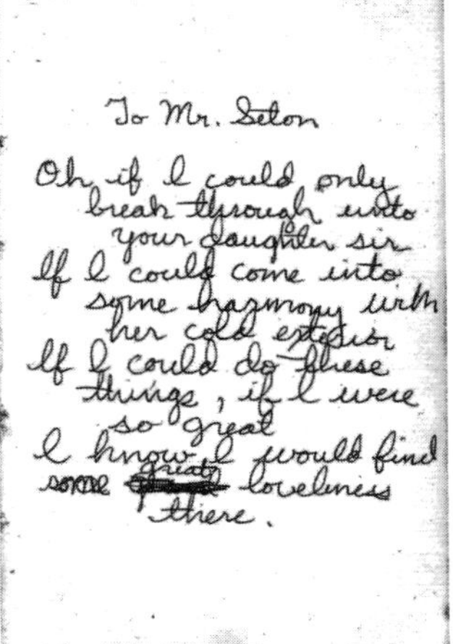

To Mr. Seton

Oh, if I could only
break through unto
your daughter sir
If I could come into
some harmony with
her cold exterior
If I could do these
things, if I were
so great
I know I would find
~~some~~ ~~giant~~ loveliness
there.

ABOVE: Poem following that to Heather Seton: "To Mr. Seton...if I could only break through unto your daughter, sir. If I were so great. I know I would find some giant loveliness there" (p. 82).

ABOVE RIGHT: "It shall have, of course, to be Paris" (see p. 77) — Rue St. Andre des Arts heading from Rue de l'Ancienne Comedie towards Rue Git-le-Coeur and Place St. Michel.

Visa Tourist
Bon pour se rendre en Iran
Nombre d'entrées ~~Une fois~~ Plusieures
Durée de séjour transit 90 jours chaque fois
Par la frontière Bazargan
Validité ~~trois mois~~ ~~une année~~
a dater du 14 ...
No. gratis ...

ABOVE LEFT: Visa to enter Iran in 1961. *N.b.,* how on the second line both in French and Persian, this visa has been tampered with. The reason is that after the author went to Iran from Israel a second time in April, 1962 (below, pp. 351-63), he did not have time to get a new visa. The above is the visa from 1961. At that point a Persian friend, he met on the bus, 'fixed' it by crossing out the "Une fois" in French and checking the "Plusieures" in Persian despite the fact it had already been previously deleted. Being a friend of the Shah and upper class, he knew how the bureaucracy worked. He then crossed out the "trois mois" in French while leaving the "une annee" in Persian. However puzzling, it worked perfectly (see p. 357: "at the border check-point at Dogobayazit").

Visas
LÉGATION DE LA RP DE BULGARIE
ВИЗА № 10160

ABOVE RIGHT: Transit visa to pass through Bulgaria a second time in May, 1961. No problem here (see pp. 89-90).

The ~~Crossing~~ into Persia

The land of Cyrus
The land of Xerxes

The road is bumpy
The road is long
Great green mountains
on either side
ringing us in
Turning into rock
cliffs, stone.

Women sitting in the
field of trees
and [illegible]
Carts with horses,
Children, the donkey
with packs

Bullocks too

The first thing is
to be completely
clean.

Look at that nice
smile
(Man with donkey)
almost hit
Something moves
me about going
through these lands.

My companions in
the bus: Venice
chatted students
Armenian, Israeli,

Herds of camels
and cattle roaming
Men spread out on
the plains

There is land to
step upon,

I know that voice
and listen to it

(Take off thy glasses
for you will
find sight.)

And follow it.

I shall be re-
created again, in
thy image,
And cross a thou-
sand deserts.

Oasis Poems

A man on a bicycle
A man walking by
the road
I chronicle my journey

A man ploughing by
the side
Donkeys with hay
The sound of the
horn
Music jangling

LEFT: "The Crossing into Persia" (May, 1961) — "The road is bumpy, the road is long. Great green mountains on either side, ringing us in, turning into rock cliffs — stone" (see pp. 91-98).

LEFT BELOW: "Oasis Poems: A man on a bicycle, a man walking by the road, I chronicle my journey. A man ploughing by the side, donkeys with hay, the sound of the horn, music jangling" (pp. 97-98: "The Crossing into Persia" continued).

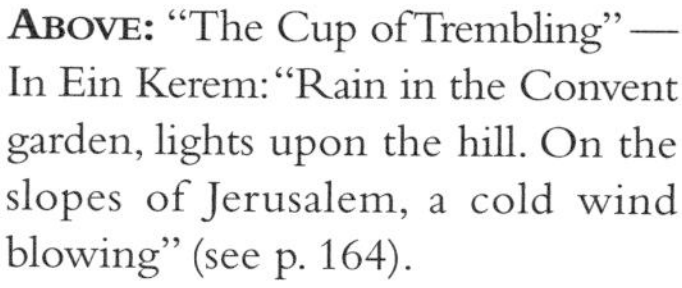

ABOVE: "The Cup of Trembling" — In Ein Kerem: "Rain in the Convent garden, lights upon the hill. On the slopes of Jerusalem, a cold wind blowing" (see p. 164).

LEFT: The Boulevard St. Germain looking towards the Odeon Metro Stop and the Carrefour de l'Odeon around the corner — "In Nazareth" (see pp. 283-302): "Paris was my love. I lay down on the grass with her, entered into her, fornicated with her, and then I left her...How I long to return to her" (see p. 294).

Above: "Tel Aviv in light — even the breakers are muffled...The Jaffa winds sooth my spirit, put it to rest...the lighthouse, the stars, the palm trees, the moon, the sky, the sea, the soft breezes" (pp. 178-81).

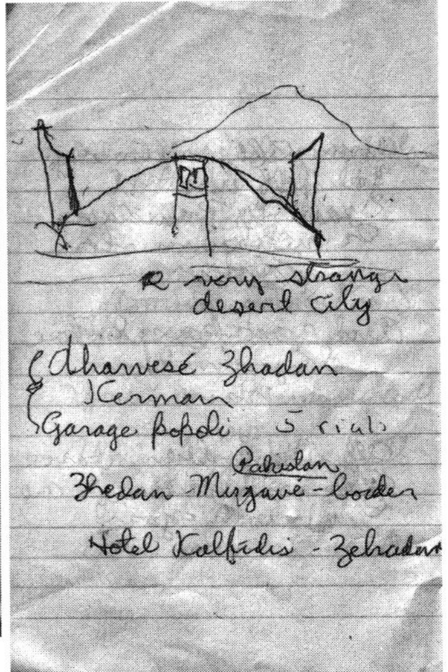

Above right: "A very strange desert city" facing the page containing the jottings about "The crap game on the road to Zahedan" and places to stay there on the next page (see pp. 376-77).

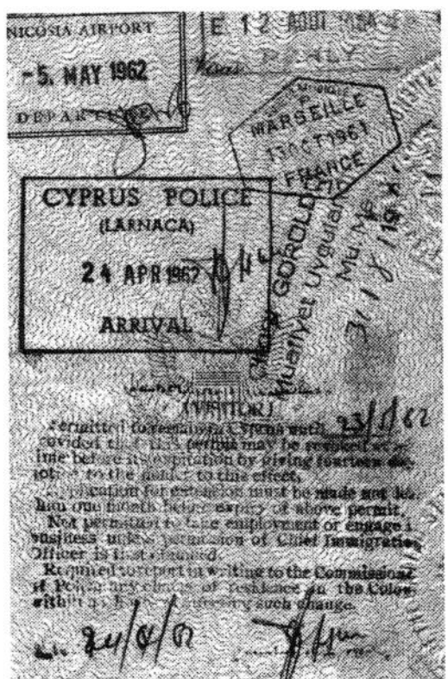

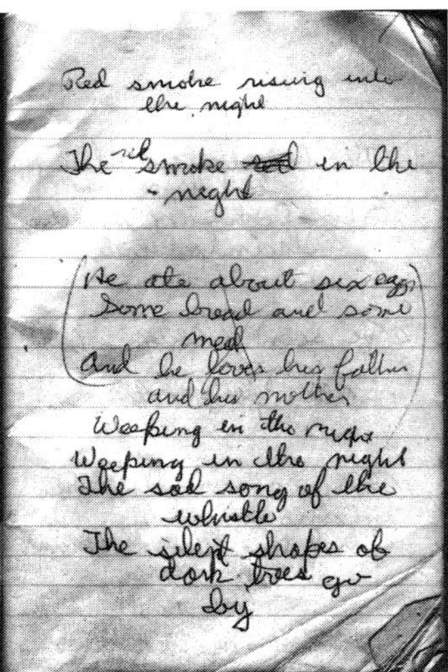

Above left: Cyprus visa, April, 1962: "Sitting on Cyprus looking at the sunset and the sun... suddenly went from soft yellow to orange in a red-imbued sky descending" see pp. (348-51).

Above middle: The sketch of a Turkish woman on the train "on the way to Erzurum" above the words: "This is right. Even being on this train" (see, p. 352).

Above right: This faces the words: "He ate some bread and some cheese, and he loves his father and his mother" and "weeping in the night...the silent shapes of dark trees going by" (see, pp. 352-3).

Above: "The rocks of Aphrodite" off the Southern coast of Cyprus on the road to Paphos (see pp. 349-58 — "Of course, the Greeks understood").

Above : Pages of the journal following "Parting from Adana" and "On the way to Erzurum."Here a sketch depicting the rising sun and"a blue ridge of mountains and another white and blue" — "on top of the world in Eastern Turkey" (pp. 351-56).

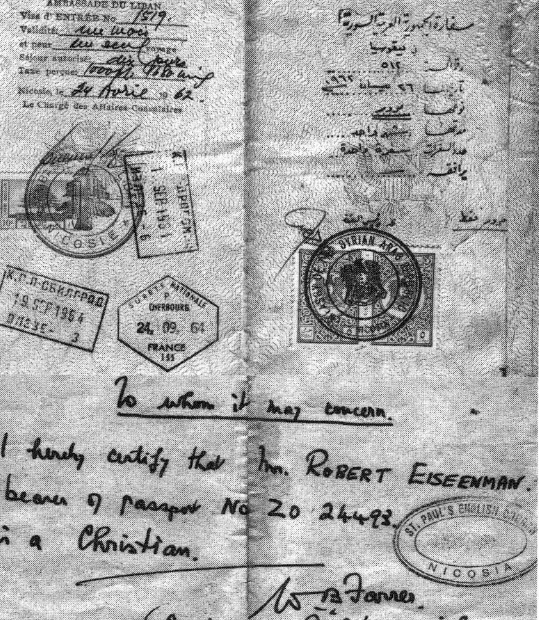

Visas
AMBASSADE DU LIBAN
Visa d'ENTRÉE No 1519.
Validité: un mois
Nicosie, le 24 Avril 1962
Le Chargé des Affaires Consulaires

Visas

CHERBOURG
24. 09. 64
FRANCE

To whom it may concern.

I hereby certify that Mr. Robert Eiseenman. bearer of passport No 20 24493. is a Christian.

W. B. Farrer.
(Anglican) Archdeacon in Cyprus

ST. PAUL'S ENGLISH CHURCH
NICOSIA

Right: Isla Seton in 1962 (see p. 334: "On Isla Seton and growing up: It is like climbing a hill and looking out until you finally get to the top and see what there is").

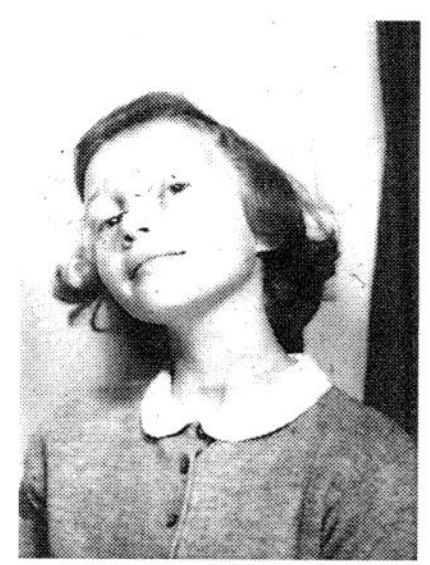

Above left: Visas to Lebanon and Syria which could not be obtained except with an affidavit that the recipient was not Jewish. This was kindly accorded me as an act of "Christian" charity by the Anglican Archdeacon of Cyprus, but in the end I did not use it — though I had actually been on the boat from Limassol to Beirut — because there had been a coup in Damascus and there were roadblocks all along the way from Beirut to Damascus. In this instance,'discretion seemed the better part of valor.' This was probably wise (though I had already been through Turkey) as my visa request in the Syrian Consulate in Nicosia had noticeably raised eyebrows — by contrast, in the Lebanese, nobody seemed to care. In the end, I flew Turkish Airlines from Nicosia to Adana, which was the reason I had no Persian visa.

Above: "The joy of Paris was that you were in no society and, therefore, could see out the windows" (see p. 362 — Harold Chapman, "View from rm. 27").

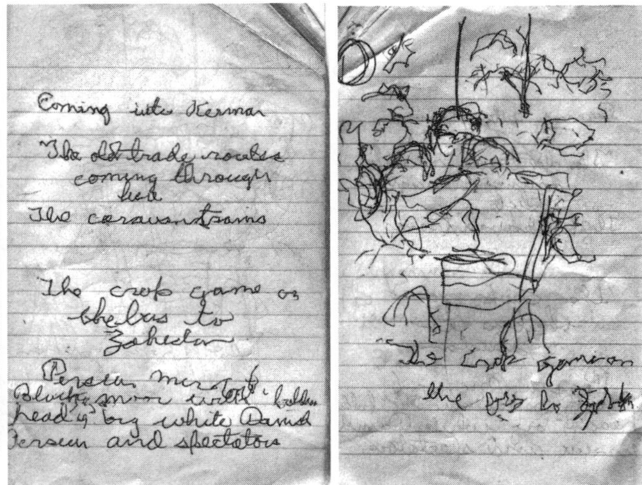

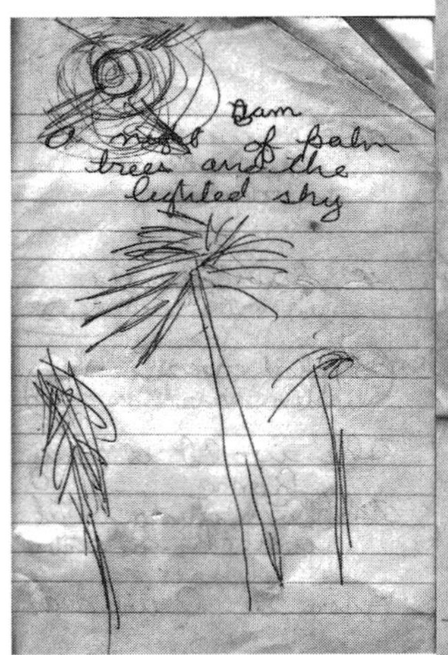

Top right: "The crap game on the road to Zahedan" (see p. 377 and note the shaky handwriting in the facing pages above because of the bumpiness of the track through the rocky desert, which most of the time was no road at all).

Above left: "Bam: A night of palm trees and the lighted sky" (p. 377).

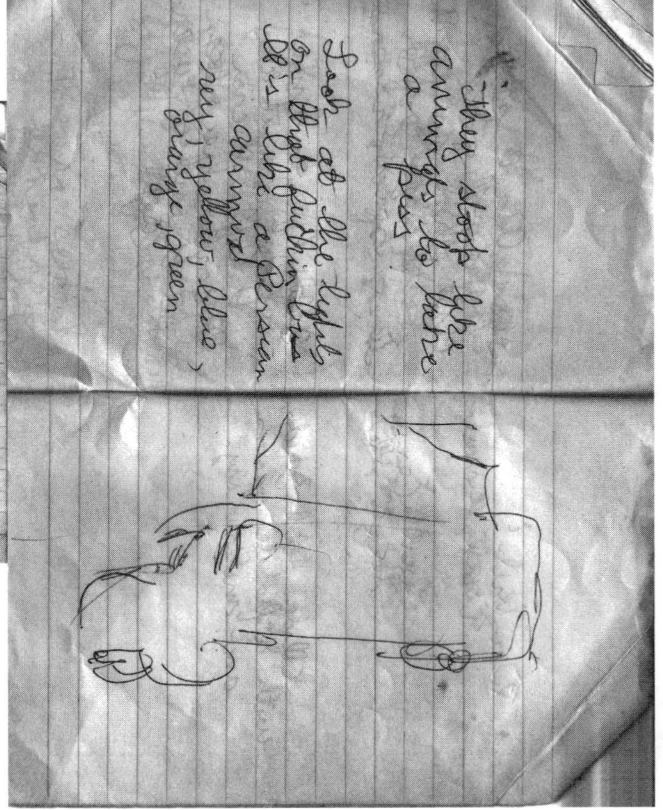

Above right: "Look at the lights on that fucking bus. It's like a Persian Carnival — red, yellow, blue, orange, and green" (see p. 383).

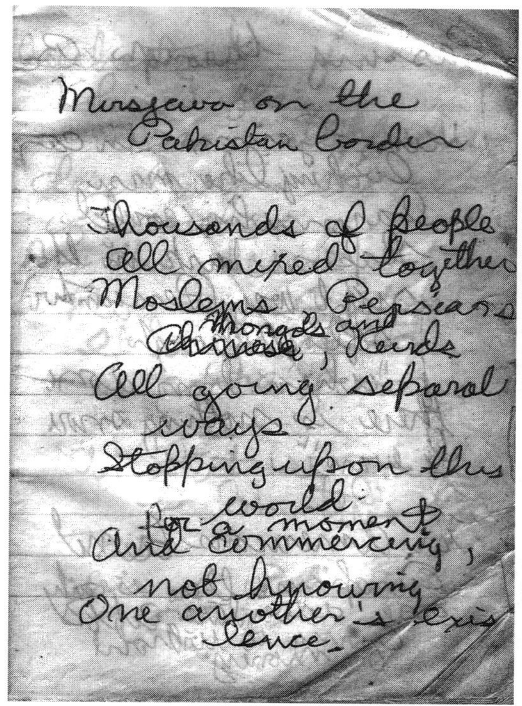

Mirsjavo on the
Pakistan border

Thousands of people
all mixed together
Moslems Persians
~~Chinese~~ Mongols and, Kurds
All going separal
ways
Stopping upon this
world
for a moment
And commercing,
not knowing
One another's exis
tence.

ABOVE: "Mirsjavo on the Pakistan border: thousands of people all mixed together: Moslems, Persians, Mongols, and Kurds all going separate ways... not knowing one another's existences" (see p. 384).

ABOVE RIGHT: See below poem: "I loved her," written after passing Nokundi on "a ghost car on the train through Pakistan, dark windows and the desert stretching wide with light" (see pp. 389-90 — courtesy, B. McNair).

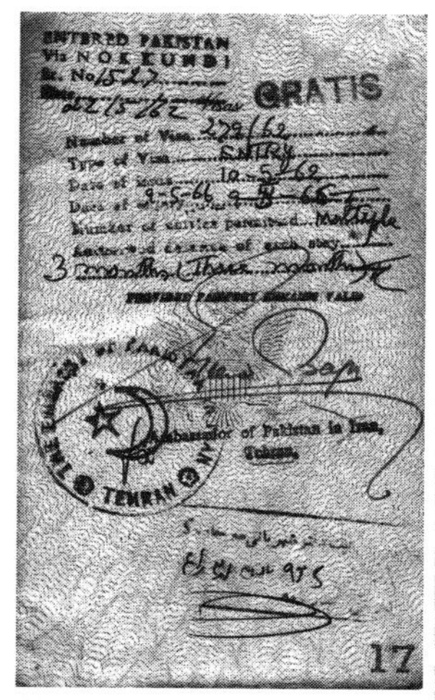

ENTERED PAKISTAN
Via NOKUNDI
GRATIS
Number of Visa 229/62
Type of Visa ENTRY
Date of issue 10.5.62
Multiple
Ambassador of Pakistan in Iran,
Tehran
TEHRAN
17

ABOVE LEFT: Pakistani transit visa issued at "Nokundi."

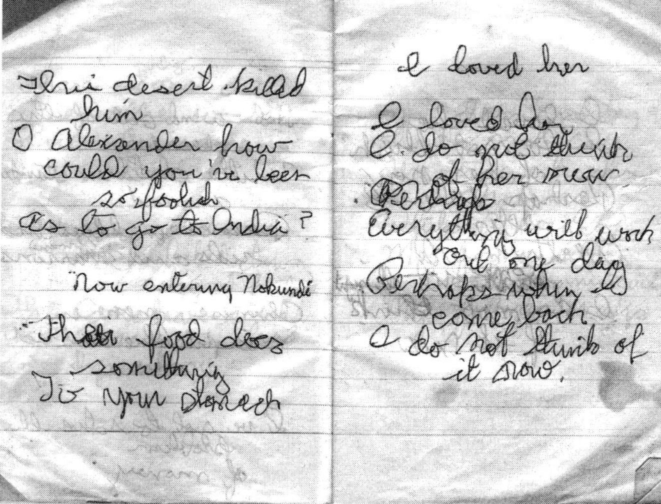

This desert killed
him
O Alexander how
could you've been
so foolish
As to go to India?

Now entering Nokundi

That food does
something
To your stomach

I loved her

I loved her
I do not think
of her now
Perhaps
Everything will work
out one day
Perhaps when I
come back
I do not think of
it now.

ABOVE RIGHT: Journal entry: "Now entering Nokundi" and on the facing page, the poem: "I loved her. I do not think of her now...Perhaps when I return. I do not think of her now" (see pp. 388-9, etc.).

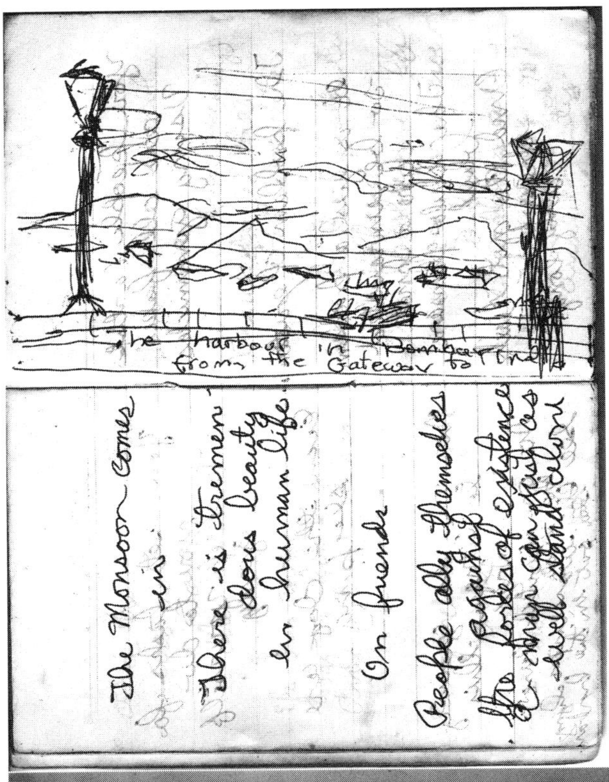

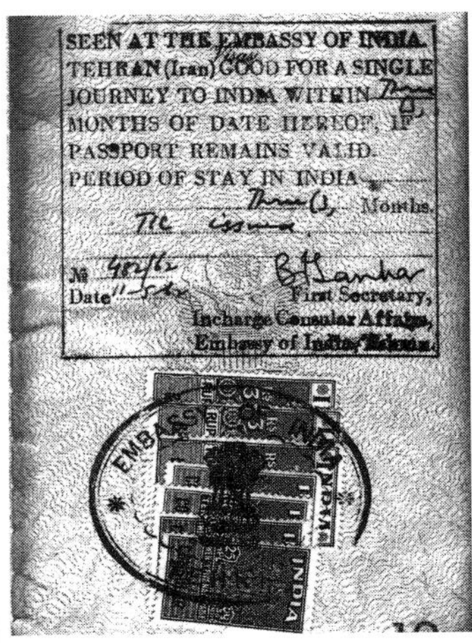

Top right: Indian visa, June, 1962.

Left: "The monsoon comes in," a sketch of "the Harbor in Bombay from the Gateway to India" (see pp. 402-423).

Above middle: Photo of author taken in New Delhi for an Afghan visa in July, 1962, because he thought he was returning "overland" (see p. 446). As it turned out, once again he did not use it because of reports of banditry along the road from Kabul to Herat, so he took the 'gentler' sea passage across the Indian Ocean (in the monsoons) and up the Red Sea (see pp. 446-53).

Left: "Egypt of the rosy sunsets, Egypt of the fires at night, Egypt of the land rock rigid, Egypt of the Sinai's might" (see pp. 452-53). A leaner, more-knowing author standing in front of the pyramids on his way back to Marseilles through Egypt via the Red Sea and the Suez Canal, August, 1962.

Work is the foundation
For doing well —
Work and something else.

How lonely I am tonight,
How I long to be off this earth.
In Paris there was no loneliness,
In New York, at home — neither.
But here, I am lonely.

There is something in this night,
As if the whole earth condensed to one —
And, then, there is India calling on the radio.

The whole world is at my fingertips.
There is some monumental strangeness in this night
Of things on the verge of happening.

"Poor girl who was so strong to love me"
— *The Chaurapanchasika.*

She was my girl, but she did not know,
She could never know.
Should she be punished like this?
Should she pay with her life?
Why Lord, if no one ever told her,
How could she know?
Does she have to go through
What I have gone through,
For that's what it takes to know
Where I have come from. No, Lord, no.

The only way
To regain your footing
Is to step out and never look back.

On hearing the radio:

There is
India calling.

The sentimentality,
What other people think.
There is a connection —
I do not know yet what.

I think I am
Beginning to resemble
My mother more than my father.

The flesh is weak.
A man can set up something to stand
While the flesh is see-sawing.
This is God.
Some men set up their businesses,
Some their fame, some their women,
Some even their bodies.
The Highest is to set up Truth.

The Lord is the way of life.
How else can we speak of Him?

The place where this should be
allowed to flourish —
It took a long time, almost three
hundred years —
Is present-day America.

On thinking of Athens:

What these men were allowed to think was
not dictated
And somehow it rose to the height of the
society,
So all men paid homage to it and sought to
do it reverence.
It governed the coming and goings of their
everyday interreactions.
Perhaps this is what is called democracy.
It was not in the Renaissance,
For there the nobility did not participate
And so it was reserved for one side of the
population only —
The artists and philosophers (not in the
center).

I am only the incarnation
Of my spirit at this moment.
How big I am is as
Big as I allow it to be,
And yet, it carries me along in time,
heals old wounds.

Men are like little ants,
Uprooted little spirits.
They kill and slaughter each other
And yet, after they are dead,
The force goes on.
Imagine to be that force incarnate —
to represent it.

Your vision
Becomes obscured by local affairs,
By rooms and women,
And old necessities like Paris,
But your destiny should remain pure.

I have had my
Enlightenment.

Problems and solutions,
Solutions and problems.

I undo the mysteries
Of this world
And find
There is nothing in them.

It is like the writhings of a dead man
Or a man in pain — a wounded snake.

It is like a snail ducking
In and out of its shell.
One's shell is one's conception of one's
self.

Which kind of man do you want to be
And which kind of morality
Do you want to show?
It is time to become him now.

I know why men
With their minds can have no peace
If they must constantly recreate themselves.

I want
To be myself,
Whoever he is.

Could you suspect
The solution before, as you went?
No, it was impossible.
Therefore one must be flexible
As one goes and not rigid,
Taking what comes, dancing —
Or else all else is lost —
Until like Jesus or Charles DeGaulle,
The solution is no longer
A part of this world.
Such is a code of honour,
Such makes a man walk right
No matter what the problem.

Nothing can end it except death
And, who knows, even then it may not end.
Is not this what the Hindus do
In preparing themselves
To escape the endless incarnations,
To become "the word" —
To go on without the body?

You fall, yes,
But then you get up again.
You come up against
Something you cannot face,
But then tomorrow comes.
You act badly, but it goes on —
There is a new day to act well.
Time goes upward, as well as
forward —
"To pyrne in a gyre," the never-
ending spiral.

I begin to
Feel it
Come back.

On the university:

O God, how much time
Did we waste doing nothing?
I think I was wise.
That far could my father see —
To the university.
I followed him until there.

I should have gotten a room after the first month.
One month with my parents was fine, even a month
and a half,
But two months, three, was debilitating.
No wonder I could not see. There was nothing solid
beneath my feet.
And to have stopped in Leicester? God knows why.
The spirit understood the necessity of it both times,
but the mind, the body not.
You should have left at that moment.
She was rapidly closing about the other thing,
But to have stayed in Leicestershire? You did not
understand.
To get back your strength never concern yourself with
things like this. It is there.
Did Leicestershire bring it back or the kibbutz —
physically, yes.

As long as we are in the jet age,
Let it be, then, the jet age.
Distance means no more than
A trip from New York to Ithaca.
A man's spirit is free —
Five thousand dollars, no more than
five dollars;
A tank of gas from Ithaca to New York,
No less than a tank from Tel Aviv to
New York. So be it.

I deserved to lose her then.
Now when I go back
It will not be for her.
It will not be the same.

On the movies:

Of course, these men play demigods.
They do not die.
Their very roles preclude that possibility.
They are our heroes.
They are men of complete action.

This is the difference
Between European and American movies.
European men are involved in human dilemmas:
The Italian dilemma — man in a sexual society.

I see my duty now very clearly,
To come to know Israel
And not to go on to India.
The money means nothing.
Do not get bogged down
In things like debts,
Old promises (to yourself),
Desires — for they enslave you.

The world is full of
Desires, wants, sins —
The see-saw of man's
Volition overturning.

How I have risen above this thing,
For daily am I gripped by the desire to hit him.
And, believe me, I have trained myself in these
months to act.
This is why "Jesus" in the end is the thing —
He lived and died it in his own time.
The gospel can only bring success.
It is but the story of this.

People will say and think
What they will.
There was honour,
But there was a Higher Way.

In the city:

Blessed be the meek,
Blessed be the poor in spirit,
Blessed be the downtrodden.

If a man wants your cloak,
Give him also your coat.
Return good for evil.

There is only one man
Who has to fight —
The coward.

I have apologized to my God.

The universe
Begins to dance around me
And I no longer around the universe.

On fighting:

I know how you feel Billy Kenny,
It's a pleasure to fight.
I never thought of it that way.
No wonder men enjoy it.
It all depends on how well
You've disciplined yourself.

Discipline —
That is
The problem of the army.

I apologize
To you Nueves,
For standing by.

You see the world is but a stage.
You must steel your nerve
To act the way you want.
You are no "Eisenman" —
You've got to be strong like Eisenman.
The die is now cast, hesitating one.
You missed your moment.
Now you must take the consequences.

Oh to be like Melvin,
        a fast cat,
Or smooth like Wills,
Or strong like Bennetts,
Or a knife like Julio
Instead of myself.
You have got to be
Strong like Eisenman.

Neither am I angry,
Nor am I frightened.
"This is an affair of honour."

What drives one
To do it is
Woman.

On his threat to "have your legs cut off":

The ending is just not consequential,
For it is not for him that you came to this
land.
This was a thing in passing.
He was a coward no matter how well they said
he could fight.
However, if he acts upon his threat,
Then you must finish it with him.
The next move is his. Let him make it.

So
I have
Turned the corner.

You see in this affair
Which was the Higher Way —
To have done nothing,
To have apologized,
To have been a "Christian man" —
This was romantic, but it was
the end.

On having hit him:

Lord, give me
Forgiveness
For this sin.

Hemingway

Who was it they buried in Idaho?
It was fit they buried him there
With the sky and the wind
And the far-flung night —
A son of America.

Who knew Idaho before?
Idaho is become holy,
Aix-en-Provence is become holy,
India is become holy,
Haifa is become holy.

PART SIX

THE RED FLOWERS ON THE ROAD TO JERUSALEM

1962

The Night Before Parting from my Room

I am going to meet myself.

One meets oneself, a former self
As he was well, shakes hands,
Knows he has returned,
Then parts.

Your whole life is
To be lived in terms
Of those few days —
Past, present, and future.
You were wounded
And following a false
path.
You could not see
The way to Persia.

The Japanese are right —
You see what the moment of enlightenment is?
You do a little thing like give up a room
And all other things begin to fall into place.

I don't know
What it is —
How an action
Creates the man.

To renounce violence,
Not to fight
And still preserve
One's self-respect,
This is something.

For the first time
It has been given unto me,
Sight — to see the blindness of others.

What you do
Upon this earth
Is not so important.
The word is "Peace."

Everything is, of course, possible.
It is a struggle.
Men's passions cause all the trouble.

On apologizing:

I believe in living this way —
I will make the gesture.
Then it will be done.

Yes,
I am a
Cosmopolitan.

Hemingway
Was looking for war.
I am looking for peace.

Up until the time of "Christ,"
Men won power through wars.

You may choose to enter Jesus' Kingdom
Or some other, for there are many —
As for me, I choose to be in his.

Through the word "Jesus,"
One comes into
The center of the universe.

I vow to put away
From my body
All pleasures
And follow
What has so long
Been neglected —
The Higher Way.

If you are going to go after women,
Then you have got to fight.
Otherwise you must not go after them.

I am beginning to understand this life.
I was walking the way I wanted
When suddenly I got into a fight.

A bearded man
Would not have
Done that.

Is this not it?
One draws oneself out
And above one's world
By cutting loose the bonds?

Poems in the Night as Uninvited Guest

On reading Oscar Wilde:

There are only two choices:
One, stay in Tel Aviv
And suffer it —
Two, go on to India.

Enough of small people —
I don't want their women.
There are enough friends to make
In all the great books handed down to
man.

It is a struggle —
Men's passions
Cause all the trouble.

I am tired of
The stage of
This Life.

The worries that destroy
A man within the city —
The fears he cannot resolve
Because he is buried within them,
Trapped to begin with.
This is why the beduin
Does not have these problems.

What does he know,
The considerations I go through?
They do not matter for him.

I see now
Why they killed "Christ" —
Of course, the two poles.
If you act to fight
Or protect yourself,
They do not kill you;
If you act in peacefulness,
They will murder you —
Still you must do it.

Notes while Reading

O Lord, it is all broken down,
It is all gone and I am forced
To wander among the ruins
Of those ageless worlds —
Among the dregs of our society,
Creating what, building what,
Laying the foundations
For some future generations
To build in splendor.
Lord, give me the strength
Not to fall in among the rubble —
To persevere and not to falter,
till my job is done.

I want to go home to New York,
I want to live, read, act, and work,
I want to lay the foundations in
The land which has got no foundations.

Thank you very much, Lord.
You have given me
Respite from my fears.
It is indeed a pleasure
To have respite from my fears.

These things
Do dot rise out of me.
They rise out of someone else.

The apology was the highest thing you did.
I shall impose my solution on him
By taking away my presence.

I want to see you father
And throw my arms about you —
And you mother too.
For out of you springs
Honour, grace, nobility — do
not stumble.

Why should I allow them to draw my blood,
Why should I place myself within their power?
I want to be at home with my parents.
I want some peace to grow strong,
To read, to develop my mind once more —
To benefit from my experience.
I know the mind of men —
Enough of grappling with daily problems,
Enough of room and board and food,
However interesting these may be — enough.
A wife, a home, a family — and then perhaps
begin again.

To India, why now? Yes now.
But I have not the strength.
"Jesus" has left me strengthless.

So you think I am mad,
So everyone thinks I am mad.
Let them think so — a man has feet.

The inside understands
More than the mind
Beholds.

I should fight with blood,
I should stay in this world
And when he comes to get me, get him.

I have solved
The Jewish problem —
Perhaps it's time to go .

Follow your feelings.
There is something
I'm following more —
The final stitch.

Believe me, there is nothing to worry about
When you believe in yourself.
In the meantime, people make mistakes —
Their weaknesses, their fears, come out,
But in belief, there are no fears.

This is
The second time
It has come.

I have intersected myself.

Character disappears
Next to God.
It is nearness, a sin.

No, I will not go out from here.
If you are to cut my legs off —
Do it, vile basest of them

Believe me,
I wanted to go,
But I will see it
Through to the end.

I have made a new friend —
Oscar Wilde.

My spirit
Is in search
Of Higher Things.

The Lord has given you sight.
What should you do with
The sight He has given you?
He has even shown you
The men who will do it.

I must go there without her,
Alone —
Bereft of her,
Who was my nemesis.

And he, too,
Is but a form
Of nemesis.

Neither shall I run
To escape my nemesis.

I have let myself down.

I know now what I have suspected
about America —
One does not live, one is enslaved,
One sees life as some motion picture
passing by.
One's feet are made of clay — one is
never in the mire.

You are building a pointless monument.
Is it necessary to build this monument?
A man either builds monuments inside,
So others cannot see or he builds them
outside,
For others to see and becomes famous.

There is a Higher Way
And you understood it then,
But it is very difficult.

He seeks the Highest Way

Do you remember Heather Seton?
Do you remember what it was to be a woman?
Do not forget or by the moment be deceived.
A woman is in the look — a woman is in the courage.

I believe in omens.
I believe in following
The thing within oneself that
Understands better than oneself.

When the symbols remain
And people have forgotten
What the symbols mean
Or from where they came,
This is dangerous.

It is strange how I understand
The ancients' religion
So completely.

The modern world is indeed
lost in chaos.
People have forgotten what
to live by.

The gods of human existence
Are the most subtle things.
We have forgotten them
Because we no longer live.
We are slaves blinded
By our work, our societies,
Bound by our professions —
And so, like Plato's prisoners,
Captives within our caves,
We never see out beyond.

These organizations,
Which have become so powerful,
Are the bonds that bind men in.
Beware of Communism,
Beware of Capitalism,
Beware of the Church —
He needs no Church,
He is everywhere,
By the land, by the sea.
Peter is the rock of Hell.
"Get thee behind me Satan."

This is why there are no more gods.
Modern man has settled down,
Become enchained, Become enslaved,
Attached to things He does not need.
When he breaks his chains, He sees his gods.

This is why the Yemenites are so well behaved
and the Chinese in New York.
Their elders have made laws — wise men have
laid down rules.
They have been followed blindly, as it were,
By the common men who see no further
Than the color of their skins — their homes.

I believe in Augustus.
What is temporal power
If it is not spiritual power?
What needs the one if not
for the other?
For society is but rules,
and laws too —
And if the one is separate
from the other,
Then is there no distinction,
No foundation upon which to
build,
No hierarchy, no wine,
But emptiness and chaos —
our democracies.

I am no good
At living alone.

What has drawn me out
Night after night?
I know it, woman.

O Spanish girl,
I'm disappointed in you —
You, for whom I thought
Honour was supreme,
You with the black hair
And green and sparkling eyes.
Perhaps it was your small body
Or the way your mouth
Curved down into a sneer,
But I thought this the
Spaniard in you —
Or perhaps your deeply
marked hands.
O Spanish girl,
I'm disappointed in you.

Why go on living on
The bare surface of events —
Why not get upon the current?

I know
It's time to
Go out from here.

On hearing long-silent music:

These things had some affect on my moods.
I was a creature of moods without work,
without discipline.
Is change possible — to where, to what?
Before there was happiness — to happiness?

These moods are very dangerous.
If you surrender to them,
You are lost.

There is a wound in my heart
Which will not stop running its juices,
Which opens and reopens in physical pain.
This wound is my heart bleeding.

I will go naked and exposed,
Sleep in a thousand streets,
Cross a thousand different lands.

All these things are dreams as you come closer,
All these things prepared you for what comes
now,
Your fights when you were young —
The enlightenment of your twenty-fifth year.

I will go down
Into the desert
On my birthday,
But not for this.

You see you have
To go on living.
Jesus did not.

In Nazareth: Poems on my Twenty-Fifth Birthday

On Reading Dante:

I don't know what it is
But people have become shades,
Their characters determined
By the home into which they are
born.
Time seems to be going by
And I seeing it as history.
Is it an honor to be welcomed
By the Senate of the United States —
Is there some highness there
Among those bulbous individuals?
I know what is the matter now.
There was nothing that was not
possible —
With her, I was going to do it,
Bring her along with me;
And now the doubt that,
Perhaps, if I have lost her,
The others are not possible either.
O why did you desert me love?
We could have done it.

Love is the softness.

Dante

If all the others
Have enthroned
their love,
Why should I not
her too,
Especially when she
Is dying for me?
Steel your nerve,
Take pen to paper,
And let your voice
begin to sing.

Ah love, you were like
The fresh-blown spring.
Why should I not tell
The story of our love —
Why hesitate I to tell
The story of your death?

I will never be
A great poet,
To seduce
The ears of men.

I know what it was now.
There was something
About her spirit, something
higher,
Something which did not
Depend upon cities, countries,
nations,
Something the others sensed
But did not understand,
Something which endows her
spirit —
Despite her ravaged body —
With the right to enter
The highest circles of Heaven.

I do not believe
I shall ever meet another.
I had already,
Without knowing it,
Wed her spirit.

What right have you to covet what
Was not yours to begin with?
You had not the choice —
You were given life.

When you meet your death,
Do not hold on to
Vain desires
And incompleted wants.

Her death is oppressing me,
Her death is upon me.
I bear it on my shoulders
For I could see and did not save her.
But there was nothing else I could do.

And then it comes like seldom
Storm clouds from across the sea
And knocks me down when I was gone
and free.
And still it oppresses me,
For she was to be at my side
All the way to Persia —
"I should not be making this journey
alone."
And now, if she were to die,
How could I go on unless
She were to be resurrected?

The Resurrection

Don't play her music to me,
For I know that she is dying,
That spirit that shall dwell
Among the shades for me —
Like Dante's Beatrice, hand in
hand,
She the other's handmaiden.
Where shall next I see her spirit
In these netherworlds of which
The poet Poe bespeaks —
His Annabel Lee, his lost Leonore?
Are you, for me, like them?
I believe you are already
Descending — being risen.

Hear the thunder clouds, it is
her wake.
The gods have come to tell me
of her funeral,
Seldom storm clouds drifting
Over the Mediterranean,
Clouds floating in from across
the sea.
Yes, they bode no good —
Some ill wind is passing.
It is her spirit — of this I'm sure.
But she shall dwell among the
higher spheres
And there shall I seek her out
to be reunited,
With the poet Dante as my guide —
His hand in mine, the two of us
with Virgil,
Our hands together clasped —
Three strangers looking at the
sun.

And there shall they lead me,
She not fit to be sweet Beatrice's
companion,
She but the symbol of our modern age,
She her handmaiden fitted only
By the wonder of her spirit —
A girl, not yet become woman,
Stolen away at her young age
By the current of our times,
Though harloted of body, pure of
spirit —
The flesh severed, aware,
Destroyed at death, unchaining the
other,
The higher, to its rightful inheritance.

Beauty is blind, for what did she know
When she stood beside him at the altar
That he would devour her? How could
she see it
When all the world sung his praises,
When all the people spoke of it as the
only way?
O what ignorance we grew up within?
How could he appreciate a such a flower,
How could he sense the rare beauty she
possessed
And how could he know his very presence
Was the asphyxiation of this scent?
And what did the bees that flew
About the honey of her understand —
Except to devour, to consume?

And she, what did she understand
And why is her nectar now running out?
O world, in which such a rare
And radiant thing is drowned —
O mediocrity, o society which knows no
stratification,
Where higher things are choked among the
lower,
Where there is no one to lift
And raise a thing to purer air
Except by one's own strength and
understanding,
Where the best is spat upon,
Drowned in spittle, offal, and sewage,
While the strongest have only to buy —
How can one do anything but condemn
you?

Ah love, you are the cruelest.
Why do you choose the frailest bond
For your habitat — it does not hold.

To John Bierhorst:

There is no doubt
You are going to succeed
While she dissipated her talent —
O thou who were far cleverer than we.

I was blessed when I
was born,
When my father said,
"For you I have no fear.
You shall be happy."
When my father said
these things,
He saw some eternal
Well of hope in me,
Some eternal love.
For this reason
I have nothing
To fear on my voyage.

There is some nobility,
Some honour, some Higher
Thing.
From the very beginning
I was conscious of it
When all the other heads
around me
Were sunken in the mud —
And even now it is so,
When these other heads
Have grown to other muds,
And still I seek it, still I
follow it,
Still my head is held high,
Still it keeps me — it is my
guide,
My mission, my honour —
What I was born for.

There are four things I could be:
Poet, philosopher-prophet, prince,
Or farmer-family builder.
Choose one and follow the Way.

I came to a deep wood
And there were four roads leading out
With numerous signposts and arrows pointing.
I followed the path of poet.
However perhaps, I thought, on second thought,
All four, performed excellently, would lead
to all the others.

What did I do — let my spirit go
Until it reached the higher air
Where it was meant to feed.
And my father, though sensitive,
kind, and just,
Was led astray by that great bulk,
America,
So he sought after material and
physical things.
But he, great soul — his suffering,
has liberated me,
Though neither of us can see —
He still within the cave of
Which the noble Plato speaks,
The distance between us
Bridged through love and faith.

I shall return and sow it up for him,
Do what he could not do —
Then go on to my nether worlds.

On the presentday novelists:

I consider
Them to be lower souls.
Divine Providence has guided me.

On Pere Gauthier's Bed
(whom I was destined to meet):

There was
Something wonderful
About reading Dante in Nazareth.

On thinking of "Jesus":

There is a right way,
But where it it?
I see it not embedded here.

Why should I live in this way?
I have lost love,
I have lost home and friends and family.
What is driving me on?
Days go by and lives grow short.
Had I been stern,
Had I coerced the flesh,
I could have done it,
But I did not do it —
And now I see my weakness
And the more I see it,
The more it envelops me.

Stop the deterioration.
Not only stop it,
But build upon it.

To my unborn son:

My son, I'm sorry —
I was on my path of destiny
And your mother could not come with me,
So you never saw the light.
Your mother held back
And I was pressed,
So you never here were born.
Forgive me son, for future centuries.

To Poetry:

For the moment I give you up, my royal
guard,
For there are generations yet to come,
Generations yet undone,
And I cannot neglect them all for you —
protect me well.

One came who was blessed
By the Angels in Heaven.

It is my twenty-fifth birthday
And I thank Him,
For I have been spared.

Paris was my love.
I lay down on
The grass with her,
Entered into her,
Fornicated with her —
And then I left her,
Freed myself from her.
How I long to return
to her.

There were three things I did not do
Which leads one to the present abyss.
Had I been dancer, lover, poet —
Fighter too — two years ago,
I could have done them:
One, calling my love;
Two, left in the month determined;
Three, gone straight to Paris by plane —
Three things I could not do,
The source of all my present grief,
And each would have brought the other.
For this, these years have not been blessed.
These present things are just pieces
To stop the dam of me.

I came to the end and
There was no way
To go.

Ah, poor one,
If we could have been united,
There would have been
A poet come forth from us,
Who would have serenaded
The Angels in Heaven.

Hello, poor one,
I do not know why but
I should not have lost you.

Ah, poor one,
How could it be that we have
Lost each other?
How could this terrible catastrophe
Have happened —
We who were so destined to be happy?
It should have been.

I went to the horse races
And for one moment turned my head —
The horses ran by.

It is like being on
The side of a mountain.

It is like coming out
From under the water
On top of the sea.

It takes courage
To jump off a moving train.
I did it once and fell.
One must go through
Much underbrush and trees
To get to the right track,
But if you want to,
You can do it.

Do not ever be afraid
To jump off the moving train
If that train
Is rushing towards your death.

It is like getting caught in the mud
Or being caught in quicksand —
Each time you must extract yourself.

There is no "right" —
One way is never to be
Lived to the bitter end.

The great man chooses life
Without compromising his ideals.
This is infinitely greater than death.

Death we are all going to do anyway.
It is how long you live and how well.

Too many people are
Too much in love with death.
Too many people are ready
To rush into things head-first.

The world is too rich a place
To die for something —
Others wish you to die
So they can be thrilled —
"Therefore choose life
That you may live"!

The sin of Jesus?

Moses was greater —
Because Moses *lived*.

Life was meant to be lived.
It is a rich thing —
Not to be dependent upon
The opinions of others.

Fools die for something
They don't believe in
And cowards depend on
The views of others
To make up their minds for them.

And above all, do not be afraid
Of the scorn of others,
For one's scorn
There is always another's approbation.
So many people have rushed to their end
For the scorn of others.

There is always another way in this world.
Time is of infinite variety —
With infinite ways.

It is like a game of dodgeball,
Cat and mouse, hopscotch —
When to jump out of the fire
At the right time,
Yet not to compromise your goals.

There are no two ways.
There is only winning or out.

I believe in winning.
The world is too rich a place
To die for something losing —
One can always become a philosopher.
Look at Plato —
Before he went down, he always got out.

Committing yourself is the thing.
Before committing, look both ways.

A Prophet like unto Moses.

To Heather:

You are my Zipporah.

You have forgotten your Lord
For other things among them.
Follow His way, of Abraham, Isaac,
and Jacob.
There is no other.

I have decided
To use physical violence —
Win or lose, it is necessary.

There is nothing in this town to
bother with.
Therefore you can keep yourself
Upon your road by staying above
it.

An Arab on seeing Haifa:

When my brothers will come
To knock all this down again.

Can you number
The windows in
That tall building?

Going back into the unknown.
There is nothing more lovely —
Like a horse riding into the desert.

He went into the unknown.

Lord I have won.
Joy, like a shaft of light,
Is beginning to creep into my life.

Go into the hills, man.
In the valleys
The people live like pigs.

There are no time limits.

There is time for all things.
Yes, my dear Heather,
I have many children now —
The Children of Israel are all
my children.

They fret and worry,
And cry, "Woe is me. Woe is me" —
Until we forget all this mamby-pamby
And become a people once again,
There will nothing great
Come from our soul.

On What the Boy from Roumania said:

Yes, they feel no responsibility
These the newborn poets —
Tossing around others' names
And beliefs as if they were their own.
Yes they are, indeed, "Beat."

An angel spoke to me
In the form of a child
And said, "Be not afraid."

On seeing a boy
And a girl
Holding hands:

It is my twenty-fifth year.

On walking on the sand:

It's like
Ithaca, New York
And walking on the snow.

All these things
Shall be my
"Passage to India."

Before you were posturing —
It doesn't matter how you sit
If your spirit is true.

There is only one thing
Which I want — a woman,
A companion on this earth
While I am here.
One's soul grows lonely.

It is time to take some step —
Give up my post, give up my room,
Eilat, Teheran, Ramat Gan, Jerusalem.
Perhaps to Alexandria?
Why not Egypt —
Have you ever seen Egypt?

Sometimes I believe
I am going into madness.
There is nothing to hold me
In this world, except my parents.

There is nothing
Necessary for you to do
When you are on your Higher Path.

Lord, give me strength,
And wipe away my past sins.

The trail left off here —
I have found myself again.
I forgot something here.
I pick up where I left off.

This feeling
Is like the surf
Which crashes over
All the little things

I know where it's leading —
In one great flood to India.

Ways, way, ways to live —
The changing of the ways.

How you ride the horse of time.

My life was charmed.
Work is not the same.
There are a hundred
Things to work for.

Passage to India

Now, as soon as time permits —
The month of March or April at the most.
Pay in this world for gifts from the other.
This journey was to be done by twenty-five.

When one grows up, one sees
There are a hundred ways to live.
If one does not, one is blind.
Money just makes things easier.

Why not use
The power of
Your money?
There is
No other way.

Everything is,
Of course,
Possible.

You pay in money
For your foolishness
Because you did not listen.

Money is fuel.

Pay in this world
For gifts from
The next.

Believe me,
There is no other way —
And so he went to Ind — i — a.

By September of my twenty-fifth year
I must return to intersect myself.
The present things are just pieces
to stop the flow of me.

A hundred thousand things
Begin to happen in my mind —
A hundred thousand ways to go,
And a hundred thousand means.

I dare
What the fates
Refuse to other men to dare.

The Setting Out

It was like a rope holding
Together the whole —
Following it, descending,
Different episodes.
Then being lifted up
And back upon the path,
Tying it together — India!

I believe I have been
Following it all along.

These falls were necessary,
The falls of your own imperfect
Nature upon a stormy sea —
You see your weaknesses?

You lost her.
It was necessary
From the beginning.

On picking up a girl:

What are you doing?
I am fucking India.

Do you remember
Those days in Paris?
They were miniatures
  of these months.

There is only
One thing to do,
One thing only —
Go on to India.

Stout heart,
Do not fail
 me now.

Destiny is
Smiling
On me.

You are
A slave
To events
And not to
Beliefs.

The Greeks were concerned
With destiny.
The gods —
The tangled fortunes of men.

I have
Experienced
The throes of destiny.

The shops are only here
For you to buy within.
O you of so little faith,
Do you forget so often?
Do you become bogged down
In these things and worship
them —
You who are only passing
through,
You upon some Higher Path?

This is my own
Private poem
Of destiny.

On the Indian yogis and
Christian mystics:

It is all right
For yourselves to do this,
But you have not the right
For your families.

An Open Letter to my Father

There is no place for me in your business.
Until now, I did not understand how far apart we
were.
And all these questions I used to ask myself —
Did you never ask yourself why a man lives?
He does not live to have a business,
To be chained to his means of employment,
So he can have nice things — this is not it.
I have seen many men now and many lives and one
is no better than another.
You may ask me to think of my children, think of
my family — I do.
I take the responsibility for my choice upon myself.
It was that you gave me freedom for, bred me for,
worked for.
I take the responsibility for all succeeding
Generations of my blood upon my own head.
The first thing they should be is men and it makes
no difference
Whether they are rich men or poor, educated men
or farming men —
They will get to heaven no quicker whatever the
way.
I take the responsibility upon myself.
You built the business up and I appreciate its rewards,
But I was not born to keep it going —
This was not why I was placed upon this earth.
No, I feel it is a slight and an inconsideration
If you do not feel this way too for, if it means so
much to you,
If you are so blinded by its temporary worth
To make of our lives a tragedy because of it,
Then I am surprised by your pettiness — and why
You should place such high hope upon a thing, a
factory, a business —
And not upon your son, I shall never know or wish
to comprehend.

For a man to work
He has to want to build
Something in one place.
There is nothing I want
To build on this whole earth.

Whatever a man wants to build,
It is possible to build —
It is simply a matter of making the choice,
Believing, and sticking with it.

Yes — a fight to keep yourself
The way a man should be.
O flesh, why were we born
So weak and with fear?

The subject of my poem:

The rebirth of faith,
And how you rediscovered your way
and smothered excess.

These things are not excess —
Excess is but a momentary thing,
Dependent on the situation at hand.

The end should have been there
And everything beyond that end
is weakness and excess.
Cut it off like an unused limb:
"If your right hand offends you,
cut it off."

You met a problem
And you could not cope with it.
It caused the hesitation
And the lack of success thereafter.

Israel was a problem,
The Kasit was a problem —
The Enlightenment of
My twenty-fifth year —
The Land was something,
But I need no land.

Because we are human,
Because we are passing,
Who can say there is no God —
And the Eternal things?
Look at the sand, the beach, the sea.

I will decide in June.

It is like solving problems —
No wonder the ancients were
So concerned with riddles.

There is only one thing
That worries me —
The pain in my heart,
My mortality.

I came to the end
And there was
No way to go.

On the boy of twelve:

What did he know about his destiny?
He could not see the ups and downs
When his eyes were blind —
He could never see.
How could he tell when to cut it off
And how could he know all these things
About the objects of desire?
And now beyond the age
Of twenty-five, where does he go?

To Mr. Ankori:

I deceived you
And, thus,
Deceived myself.

On Anne Ettenberg:

I found in this
A sign
To guide me on.

By the gods that live on High,
By the gods that live down below,
This is a strange and marvelous universe.
If you come out of your cave,
If you throw off your chains,
You have no idea
The wonders there are to behold.

To stake out
Your consciousness —
For whom are you performing?

A vision has been afforded you.

Venus
Kept leaving
Her hair for me.

It is necessary
For you to know
How to kill.

The history of the world
Also disintegrates.
This is the time for power
to be held.

I have seen angels, gods, and men.

How happy I am
For I feel all the cares of the world
Lifting from my soul
And, once more, I feel the coming of spring.
I remember days spent in the field above the lake —
The daffodils, the buttercups,
The long blue lake stretching away.
Four years and I have not felt that feeling,
But still it is there.

On writing a letter to my father:

Do not send it.
Let time
Take its course.

The ship of life goes on.

If you do not waiver,
If you believe in your God,
You can have any woman you want.

Shall it be
To Singapore by sea —
Or overland?

Pursue India and forget about these people
And everything will be all right.
However, if you pursue these people
And forget about India, then you will be in Evil.

Do not listen to their voices,
The sweating hands,
For the spirit and flesh are weak —
But proceed upon the path to India.

Yes, I feel
My strength returning:
"Come home now!" — "Passage to India."

It was not your girl
Who destroyed you then.
It was your parents.
You should have heeded
Your brother's warning.
It was heaven-sent —
You mixed up the two.
She freed you.

Poor, foolish boy who could not see.
You are very blind sometimes.
They wished to pull you
Down into their pit.
Forgive me Lord —
If they are sinning must I sin too?
Yes, if you are taking their money.

To honor is not to become a slave.

He is the Lord of Abraham,
The Lord of Isaac,
The Lord of Jacob —
And the Lord of Eisenman.

March 15th, 1962:

"No one remains prosperous
For very long" — Herodotus.
All history passes away
And there is only this.

They are all going
In that direction
Called "America."

On seeing a tough-looking fellow:

They are fighting unseen devils
While the world passes them by.

There is no straight way to go.

I feel like Alexander cutting the Gordian Knot.
I am no poet content to dream of things.
I did not sing my love and then not take her.
Before all things, even a poet, I am a man —
a man of destiny?

Woman is reflected light, woman is the moon,
Woman is the Garden of Eden,
Woman is the impetus for the society of man.
Woman does not see the light of men,
Woman sees her position — the reflection of
others.
The artist, who sells present life for future
renown,
Is the only one who carries his own light
within himself.
In former times, it was the hero,
But modern society has enslaved the hero.
Therefore the artist and the hero have switched
places.
Owing to the impotizing organizations
Of man — communism and democracy —
"Cutting the Gordian Knot" is cutting
The whole society of man with a sword.
It is not longer possible without destruction.
Men and women have sown the seeds of their
own destruction.

On the sweater knitted for me by my cousins,
Burned after their lack of hospitability,
And the suitcase mended in Erzurum:

I wish I had that sweater now and that suitcase.

There is
The Big Dipper.
How beautiful
It looks tonight.

The Red Flowers on the Road
to Jerusalem

Even here — on these barren hills
you are my hope.
You grow untroubled by the
hurricane winds.
Here, there — among the vineyards,
Breathing the unpolluted air,
You are my apotheosis.

And the child came running after me
And I did not wait for her.
There are so many moments like this
Wasted in senseless motion.

On seeing a dog barking:

You do not prove anything scientists
When you prove there are no spirits within.
These things are inside men's minds —
I offended the spirit within.

I have not felt so peaceful a long time.
There is nothing in my way now,
There is nowhere I want to go —
The end of cares, the coming of bliss.

You don't know
What it is to experience
A Middle Eastern spring.

This is truly
The country
Of the Lord.

Believe me, Lord,
There is only
You and I.

It flows over all things
Like a soothing flood
And bathes them in forgetfulness —
Time's consciousness.

Bending my spirit
To fit my will:

I'm going down
To Eilat tomorrow.

The Lord has sent me a fever
To lift me out of this city —
          Passage to India.

The Lord said,
There would be other ships —
Yes, and there were.
Ships going every month,
Many ships.

Yes, it's necessary
For me to go to India.
No, it's not the right time to go.
I will go to india on
The fifteenth of April — next month.

Put the charm and grace
Back into your life —
Go to India not Singapore.

I think it's better
To go overland
Next month.

I was serving
A Higher God
All the time.

All these defences,
All these strengthenings,
All these purposes,
All to serve the Higher God.
To others I seem mad —
Passage to India.

On the Orange Blossoms outside
Petah Tikva:

Into even the worst events,
The gods are blowing perfume
So all is clothed in ambrosia,
An aphrodisiac of their breath.

The winds of charm return.

Hope is the charm.
When you have hope,
Nothing you do can be wrong.
There is no struggle —
They cannot knock you down.

I like to be out on the Land — like a
Thoroughbred horse — free and running,
With the great white wind for my rider
And the great wide sky for my mane.

Do not hold me down to nations,
Do not hold my spirit upon lands —
My spirit rests in no country.

Are there some desires
Which are constant?
What things are not blown away
By the every-removing time?

On the Radio

The Voice of America,
The Voice of Russia —
Though near in time,
Far away in space,
Disappearing like
Rome and Persia.
Other voices coming.

On Isla Seton and growing
up:

It's like climbing up
A hill and looking out
Until you finally get
to the top
And see what there is.

Everybody thinks they know what to do,
Everybody thinks they know what *you* should do —
Societies, governments, ways of life.
But a man is free, unless enslaved by other men —
Do you realize what this means?

A man gets
A hundred chances
To do it right.

There's no trick to enter the Kingdom of Heaven
After giving up the things of this world:
Desires, appetites, women, friends.
The trick is to enter it *in this world* —
With fucking, family, and responsibilities.

I was a man
Locked in fear.
I begin to
Unlock myself.

I must learn to
Fuck without passion
And fight without fear.

A man must have confidence.
He must have confidence and
He must act what he believes.
Even in the face of utter
Complacency and indifference,
Never say, why bother? Bother!

I do not know what these breezes do to me.
There is a softness, some rich balm.
All my dreams are centered in them.
Yes, it's time to go —
I hear their echoes in my soul.

There is
A peacefulness
Spreading over all my past.

That great sprawling metropolis
Known as "America,"
That seething mass of people —
I am content to see movies about it.

My spirit is like a musical instrument —
It needs to be played in tune.
It is a chord of music
With no existence apart from the listener.
My spirit is a little bird that sings,
Dancing from tree to tree.
It does not exist apart from
The people, places, and things is sees.

In Honor of Keats and the Sweet New Style

I am a soft bird dancing,
Dancing from god to god,
from land to land,
Dancing from Apollo's hand,
Dancing to to Yahweh's head,
Dancing to "Jesus"' sweet name.
And whom shall I lift on high,
Whom shall I praise supreme,
The gods of India? Or should
I like a little bird
Flit from tree to tree?

You sharpen
Yourself
By experience.

At the Dan Bar The Waiting Room To Hell

No wonder
All the world
Loves an actor,
No wonder
All the world
Loves a play —
All these fakes
Sitting around
In their
White uniforms
Like virgins.

O Lord,
Why have You placed us here
To play this act?

A man's spirit is free.

Change the scene,
Change the act!

All of these deceptions are played
Because of the stupidity of mankind.

Whatever you want,
Just go and get it —
But choose your ends High.

No one knows what anyone else is —
It is all an act anyway.
The spirit is free and open,
And knows not the condensations of
personality.

Look at the end
And you know
The man.

The thing to do is
To do it better than they
Without betraying yourself.

However long it takes,
Then this is —
However long it takes.
There is time.

India is the completion

Be persistent —
What, back again?
So they see him again.

The injustice
Of the world
Is immense.

I have no more
time
To throw away
on it.
Ready or not,
It's time to act.

Hold on —
There is
Nothing to
Hold on to.

Plans are nothing.
Plans are made
To be broken.

It is necessary to impose your word
with physical force.
Money is just the substitute for
physical force.

They will
Never know
How right I was.

It is a very strange land —
But seeing you in the spring like this,
With your cloak of green,
Takes off your mystic attraction.

So this is the way of life —
Violence, killing,
And blood.

Do not go into his cafe.
There will be time
For him later.

Yes,
You've got
To lie to them.

The evil of Jesus Christ is the Church,
The Church is the evil thing of the Gentiles.
That is why it is in Rome.

I shall rebuild the Lord's Temple in Jerusalem
And "Jesus" shall be enthroned therein.

The Church in Rome
Is the evil thing of the Gentiles.
I shall rebuild the Lord's Temple in Jerusalem.

To the Gentiles:

You are "grafts upon the tree."
Well, the tree is growing again!

On an incident in Syria:

Do you hear the rifle fire?

On modern man:

Why do they not
Have need of gods?
Because they are slaves —
And sometimes I too.

Lose, lose, lose,
But there will come
A time when I shall not lose.

I draw my strength,
Not from my family,
But from the gods —
The gods, the multiple
Variations of the One,
the Lord.

My heart swells with joy.

Everything planted
Is beginning to sprout again —
Everything is coming back.
I feel like weeping,
I feel like crying,
One does not work for nothing,
One does not sow for naught.
The field planted begins to
sprout.
O know ye, the Lord is good.
His mercy is everlasting,
And His Truth endureth to
all generations.

Believe in Me,
For I am the Lord thy God,
The Lord strong and mighty,
The Lord of Hosts.

To kill a thousand devils.

Gather your energies,
Give praise to the Lord —
His hope has returned.

I spit myself out,
I recreate myself —
Passage to India!

There is my star.
This time it
Is Venus.

Sunset on
The Mediterranean —
Black hills at night.

People in the car:

Arab woman with child,
Jewish driver,
Two Sephardim talking —
And me.

PART SEVEN

THE PURPLE HILLS ON THE WAY TO ISFAHAN

1962

Beginning on Cyprus

On seeing the blood-stained
clothes in the Nicosia
police-station:

(Two Turkish journalists
were shot last night
with thirty-three and
thirty-four bullets in
each body respectively)

The end of man
Is nothing.
All his desires,
All his pride,
His finest clothes,
End up in this:
The shedding
Of his blood.

The question is whether
A man is willing to
Submit himself to the law
Thereby losing himself.

Cy—prus

I've come to Cyprus to win back
My goddess of love,
Aphrodite.

On seeing the Rocks of
Aphrodite:

Of course,
The Greeks understood.

At the Fontana Amorosa

On seeing the tourist litter
in the limpid pool:

The squalor of human life —
A long white, naked arm
inviting me in,
And the fountain — this is
civilization.

O Aphrodite,
The world of gods,
The world of men — forgive me.

Land of green fields and brown —
Hills checkered like California.

A child sitting here
And people working —
The smell of fields dry in
the sun.

Sitting on Cyprus,
Looking at the sunset,
And the sun,
Like an augur's stone
Suddenly went from
Soft yellow to orange
In a red-imbued sky,
Descending.

The Close of Day

This is my soul —
The rest are pictures:
The sun sinking like
A coin of prophecy
into the sea.

Cyprus:

A grapevine and the stars at
night.

The night sky
Full of cloud.

Parting from Adana

The whistles
On the platform shrill —
The whistle of
The train in the sky.

Turkey:

A land of mountains and plains.

On the Way to Erzurum

There's the Euphrates —
The end of the Euphrates.

This is right,
Even being on this train.
I don't know how —
I intersected myself.

Asia Minor

What a pity,
What a rich land
It could have been — the Lydians.

Before the sun goes down,
Before going to sleep —
I loved somebody once.
I don't think ever again.

Stopping by a town
With the sun going down,
Black half moon and
White star upon the window
Against the speckled land —
The smoke red in the night.

He ate six eggs,
Some bread and some cheese,
And he loves his father and his mother.

Weeping in the Night

Weeping in the night,
The sad song of the whistle,
The silent shapes of dark trees going
by,
The bright stars, the cool breeze —
The lights of another hundred towns.

I've seen enough
Of the way
Other people live.

Blue clouds
In the morning
And the land opening up.

Erzurum

Erzurum in the morning
Is like a Siberian town,
The snow-skinned mountains,
The gray smoke rising,
The black birds, the crows, the
trees full of nests,
The smell of soot in the crisp
chill air —
It's as if the spring never comes
here.

Going into the
end of the world
in Eastern Turkey:

The land so great,
And the black and angry sky,
The endless green —
And not a cow in sight.

On thinking of
filling up
the girl:

That is what
I like doing
More than
Anything else
In the world.

The black sky at
The top of the world —
The endless rim of
White-topped mountains.

Even though I don't
Have the money,
I'll do it the right way.
I don't know why
I had to come
All the way round
The world to prove it.

The world is my home,
The land, the woods,
The trees upon it —
Every town and every
street.

On top of the world
in Eastern Turkey:

A blue ridge of mountains —
And another white and
blue.

I put her out of my mind.

They certainly knew the world —
The ark coming up here
Among these hills
And topped by Mount Ararat.

With mother on the
day of parting:

Never forget
The tragedy
Of that moment.

There's the road —
I see it ahead
Through green hills.

At the Customs Check-point
at Dogobayazit

Men's cannons to make war
Are dwarfed here,
And look like little toys
Beside these hills.

Mt. Ararat
Covered in snow —
And the green,
Himalayan grass.

The world is just sitting on the edge waiting —
All philosophies have been picked clean.
There has got to be come some new ideology
To shake it at its very foundations.
Even I am being colored by it —
A universal kind of Hellenism has appeared
With the language English and the style French.

A bird sitting on a wire
In the middle of
Nowhere.

Persia

A camel waving her tail.

The herds of camels
And cattle mixed —
The herds of donkeys.

Houses
Climbing out
Of the plains.

Long green prairies,
Turning drier.

Mt. Ararat
And her sister,
White in cloud,
Reaching skywards.

River beds drying up.

The spacious mountains
In purples, blues, and greens,
The wind blowing across the valley —
Or dust, not interrupting their serenity.

It is not here.
What is not here?
"*Om*," Eternal Perfection —
Everything.

All because she
Had promised herself,
She was going to do it.

The ends of man are so petty —
And why one generation
Cannot destroy
What another has built up?

In the steps of Plato's
Republic
Two thousand five
Hundred years later —
With the world and
Not a single city-state,
In order to raise life
To its highest degree.

On the holding of wives in common:

Our present system reduces women
To the status of slaves
And men to the status of bondservants.

On violence and the breaking of the
chains,
All deduced from an observation of
the nature of men
On the verge of a great emergence,
or destruction.

On Communism and the Method of Reducing
Men to State Slaves:

Everything is training —
Take a man who has seen no other thing
And he will be no other thing.

The joy of Paris was that
You were in no society
And, therefore,
Could see out the windows.

There was something in me
which had died —
It is like striking matches.

There are a hundred cities
And a hundred worlds to live in —
And a hundred people to live with.

I am recovering myself.

Garden Music in Teheran — Fragments from a Perfumed Dream

In the gardens of Teheran
Beneath spacious green mountains,
Crowned in white snow even in summer,
With the cool, delightful fountains
And the nightingales' ceaseless singing;
I saw my destiny spreading out before me
And the week in Teheran — sweet rain
With the whole movement of my life —
Part predicted, part predilected,
Going towards a certain end.

What is this that's spreading over —
White incense of purple clover,
Like some sweet rain, like some soft cloud,
Sweetly clothing my existence
With the white-bodied, black-winged tanager?
Did you not always know of its existence,
The soft odors completely pervading,
Balm for India's ceaseless fever?

Hear the softness of the fountain
With the water's ceaseless flowing,
And the sounds of children playing,
And the nightingale's perfumed song.
Black and white magpies hopping,
Insects buzzing, white peace doves,
The Garden of Eden — delirium.

The Jews and the Indians

Now you know the different yearnings —
One is space and soft enchantment;
The other, work and desert insulated
from impureness.

On a Street in Teheran

There is the father
Of my life,
Looking down and over things.

A night in Teheran —
The clouds,
The happiness.

Night
And stars —
On to India.

On turning off
the alarm on my clock and
not catching the bus to Kerman:

No, I didn't get up.
I didn't go yet,
I'm freed of it.

I don't believe
In going anywhere
At five o'clock
In the morning.

On Tel Aviv

There was no life possible there,
So why should you have bothered
Prophesying to them on the streets?
The Hell with those old people —
This is something completely new.

No, tomorrow I'm not going to go.

Then, if I don't
Go this week,
I will go next.

I put down
The ringer
On my clock,
Because I
Did not feel
Like going
Tomorrow.

On thinking of my
father's business:

What meager things
His spirit feeds upon,
What poor books he
reads.
O people, do not look
so low,
There are higher things
For the eyes to see,
To possess, to pass on.
Better be like a
simpleton
And sit like a fool
Within the garden
Looking at the water.

My father's business is as dead as Paris —
I love him, but I cannot fit
Into his clothes.

I long ago threw away
My old clothes —
Those society painted on me.

You have to make
A hundred decisions every day
To keep yourself going
In the right direction
And, then, break the,
Like a sailing vessel
With the cool breeze,
In order to sail along
The swell-course of your spirit.
Otherwise, you will lock in
Upon a hundred troubled things.
A poet makes a hundred
Decisions every day
To keep the course
Of his spirit right.

An Apology

Perhaps it is not so
Beautiful as some others,
Perhaps there are others
With loftier song
And sweeter voice,
But it is my song.
Had I been born with
The nightingale's voice,
I would have done it
better.

The human spirit is like
A sowing machine, a
dovetail block,
A needle and thread.
A being wanting to love —
Incomplete, it fills itself
up
With its own conceptions.

They do not know,
They are not in possession
Of their own spirits.
The only thing that wins them
In the end is — with certainty.

You go into the "Kingdom of Heaven" —
Does not every woman like to think
She possesses the Kingdom of Heaven?
She does.

They build it up so big
It begins to dominate your very mind
And so becomes an obsession.
I am free and on my way again.
I can sing about what I choose.
O you capturers, here's to the liberators.
The poet is free of this very world.

There is nothing I have to do.
I'm free.
There is always another day to
do it in.
I could have stayed in Teheran,
And India is there with girls
And love and more mirages.

There, it has come back
And it will not stop until the end.
The girl is gone,
But the spirit is still there.

Bus to Kerman

This is going to be
An interesting trip —
Bus decked gaily with
Tree leaves and flowers.

Don't worry about money —
A way will open Up
Through the Red Sea.

So begins the desert —
To be conscious
Of mortality.

In the bus:

Every time
Upon starting —
A prayer.

The Purple Hills on the Way to Isfahan

To go on, to experience,
To embrace things,
Not to hold back —
This is always the thing.
There is something
Excellent about this thing.

Joyce died
And became lost
In his own style.
Hemingway's art
Was insufficient
To express
His feelings.

What a beautiful town —
A story-book town,
Walled upon the plains
Between two mountains.

Clay brick dwellings,
Inlaid mosque dome,
Rice and moat —
And children washing.

Home alone in the desert
With blue mosaic dome
And geyser sprinkling.

Isfahan

On the banks of the
Zahande River
in Persia:

It looks like India.

The Persian desert is
Black in the morning
When the sun comes up.

The shadow
of the bus:

It looks like
A ship alone
In the desert.

The neat patches of houses
With Middle Eastern domes —
The purple crags of mountains.

The wind out of the desert.

You are letting
A whole desert go by
Without comment.

People passed through here
In search of riches,
But nothing worthwhile
Ever came out of here.

Letter to an Unknown
Friend

To persevere in the
face of all —
This is the thing.
To be decisive
Is not so important —
Only for the moment.
Indecision is not so
terrible.
The next day comes.
But to know what
You want and
Where you are going,
This is the thing —
And to persevere.

The jagged mountains
Sitting upon
The mist
Of the desert.

You are thinking very well now.
You've got the full capabilities
Of yourself once more at work.
You left on the day you felt like it,
Train to Zahedan or no train to Zahedan —
And you passed those days in Teheran.

All right then, Voice,
Keep on guiding me —
I'm with you.

Yazd

A very strange desert city.

Coming into Kerman

The old trade routes
Coming through here —
The caravan trains.

The crap game on the road to
Zahedan:

Persian merchant,
Black moor with balding head,
Big white Danish-Persian —
And spectators.

Bam

A night of palm trees
And the lighted sky.

A cat went into
The water pool
To drink.

A plain of rocks.

Stopped over here
Until the sun
Goes down

The world is my home
And everything in it,
Which separates me from it,
I will discard —
And let the time go by.

Everyone has his own personal
dignity.
In the West, everyone behaves
like rats,
They completely enslave each other
to a way of life.

I do not bemoan the fact
I have to die —
I know this will come,
A fitting end.
But, while I live,
I want to do it better.

Give me the strength now
To become what I want to be.
Take away this deep weakness
That shows itself in my face, my speech.

Democracy
Enslaves
Mankind.

My penis is as long as
The countries
I've traveled through
And as powerful as Israel.

This desert is
The last link,
The end of all
My former selves.

A black desert.

On meeting people:

It is as if each one is predestined.

In the desert
between Persia
and Zahedan:

There
Are things
Growing again.

This is the dividing line
Between Europe and India.

To drink of water.

Nothing rotten to
Destroy this book.

Mounds
With plants
Growing on them.

You are hooking
Into your new life
By the slightest link.
That it should all
Come down to this.
You are holding on
To your old life by
The slightest thread.

This is certainly,
Without doubt,
A passage to India.

Those black stones are all gone
And there is sand,
And soft brush is now present.

Duzbub!
(with a smile),
Robert Eisenman, May 20th, 1962.

I don't even know
The day I left Teheran.
It could have been
A hundred years ago.

They stoop
Like animals
To take a piss.

Look at the lights
On that fucking bus.
It's like a Persian
        carnival —
Red, yellow, blue,
Orange, and green.

Kalfidas Hotel, Zahedan —
With a white moon
And lighted sky.

Christianity, that is
An impossible doctrine,
Whether one believes it
Or believes he does.

Ecstasy I don't know,
And I don't ever wish
    to know either.

Mirsjavo on the Pakistan Border

Thousands of people all mixed together,
Muslims, Persians, Mongols, Kurds,
All going separate ways —
Stopping upon this world for a moment
        and commencing,
Not knowing one another's existences.

PART EIGHT

PASSAGE TO INDIA

1962

Heinz — German in the car,
Looking like a Prussian officer,
Who could slap a Turk in the face
In the right way — Persian too —
And get away with it, softened
though:
"When I'm done, there's nothing
more I want."

For Americans and Europeans,
There's only one adventure left,
Going it without money.

Kohi-Tuftan

Train stopped
In the desert
In the middle
of nowhere.

This is Pakistan now.

There is one city
In the world —
And its name is Paris.

In Pakistan

A hot wind out of the desert
With children standing around,
Dressed in blues, reds, and marrons —
Turkomens in light blue and red.

The two Germans
Hitchhiked down —
national pride.
The Canadian tried.
The American had
dysentery.

I've got to solve
The problem
Of money.

The desert killed him —
O Alexander, how could you
have been
So foolish as to go to India?

Now entering Nokundi.

Their food
Does something
To your stomach.

I loved her

I loved her,
I do not think
of her now.
Everything will
Work out one day.
Perhaps when I
return —
I do not think
of her now.

For days and days,
I do not care,
The train keeps
moving,
While I forget
My former ways,
My former cares,
My former self.

I could go by train to Karachi,
I could hitchhike —
Either way I do not care.

My companions in the car — a ghost
car on the train through Pakistan,
dark windows and the desert
stretching wide with light):

Canadian drifter — thin whiskers, not
yet man,
American — big fellow, Californian, lost,
German — Heinz, going to Amman to
see the headhunters,
Foolish, crazy, but very likeable,
And Horst, old Gotterdammerunger sort,
but very typed.

American, didn't like to sleep outside;
Canadian, torn between hitchhiking
And not — Germans, both insane.

A Dream

I see a whole band of people marching
Along in time with the rhythm of the train,
Beating on tambourines, singing this song —
My cousins, my friends, the peoples
In every city and country in the world.

If the West
Does not destroy the East,
Then the East
Will creep into the West.

They treat each other like pigs,
The poor throwing upon
The poorer ones — like dirt.
It is this that permeates their
whole society.

This land
Is inhabited
By other peoples.

On the Way to Karachi

There is no point
In not eating.
Twice in Iran
You did it badly —
The rest you did well.

Can one climb to the top of
A mountain one cannot see?
A man is only as big as
The end he sets for himself.
Do some men walk into
The unknown every day,
Putting their trust only in
the Lord —
This is the way of the prophet —
Or do they go only as far as
they can see?

I've given up
Worrying about the water.

Coming into Siby, Pakistan —
the hottest place in the world:

A hot wind blowing out of India.

You are doing things very badly.
Let it go out of your hands,
Let it go into the hands of the
One.

The Indus River Bridge,
the Arabian Sea.

Palm trees and a hawk.

On seeing a dark child
with a dark father
outside Karachi:

The human being
Comes into this world
In complete bewilderment.

Karachi

There is
Something about Karachi
That reminds me of Tel Aviv.

First camel-drawn
Cart I've ever
Seen.

In a Western house:

No wonder
They're so sterilized.
They boil everything out.

You are a fake, a phoney —
They are tying you up in
little knots.

By the Port in Karachi

I crossed
A long desert
To get here —
And now I'm on,
The other side
Of the desert.

The sounds of the sea
Are like no other sounds —
Voices, tom-toms, singing
Out of Africa and India.

In Karachi, Pakistan by the sea,
I took some decisions
That were going to affect
The future course of all my days.

Through a hundred darknesses I would
not fear.

How blind the world is,
How little the people
Who compose it are.

Is not the caste system of India akin
to Plato's *Republic?*

Passage to India

Messageries Maritimes,
British Orient Line clerk
At the end — Pakistani:
"We are in it now."

The Fight against Barbers

I cannot see the back of my head,
So I cannot cut my hair myself,
But for months and months now
I have been trying to get
My hair cut the way I want it —
I thought this problem only in
America.

On theft, killing, and seduction:

If all these things are broken down,
There's something else which
Holds the spirit up.

As long as I'm dishonest,
The Lord denies me women.

On seduction:

It's like playing chess —
Waiting for the opening,
Then jumping in, and checkmate.

But if I'm jumping after clouds —
If I'm lying down and
They are floating by,
Where then is the One?

On buying friends:

The new American position in the world.

Ship to Bombay

One debt to pay off
And everything will
Come out all right.

The decisions you make
Only have the effect
Of molding reality.

The Problem of Money

(Written on the deck of the boat in Karachi, Pakistan, sleeping on the red, green, yellow and many-spangled blanket with the sounds of the port, the lights, the tall cranes):

Money is just fuel
To keep you going.
You can use as much of it
Or as little as you like.
Depending on how clever
you are,
You will get there with
More or less difficulty.
But this is not the thing.
The thing is to get
There pure in spirit —
With a pure conscience.
Otherwise, there was
No point in going. Money
Is just one of the things
That has to be surmounted.
You can bang your head
Against the wall and
Every night, every day,
Go against it (for some this
becomes
the supreme achievement)
Or in the end you can pay —
But then it has to be
Be your own money.

These people are no
More foreign to me
than Jim Harper
(a white Anglo-Saxon
Protestant friend
from college) —
And I to him.

To an unknown American girl whom I heard
they would not allow to go third-class
from Mozambique to the Seychelles, and
the worn-out, middle-class American male,
who tried to help her, counciling moderation:

As soon as time sweeps all these people away,
Then there will arise a new race of Americans,
Native, proud, athletic, strong —
Mixing with each other on the trains,
In the coffee houses, on the seas —
Drawing strength from one another's courage.
And, if for a moment we stumbled,
If for a moment there were a lot of heart attacks
Because we did not know which way to direct our
energies.
If for a moment the soft life overwhelmed us —
Not for long, because we don't need them,
Not the comforts nor the protections.
And I'll tell you why we are recovering,
Because down deep we're strong,
Down deep we're tough, down deep we're pioneers,
Down deep we'll go anywhere, do anything —
anytime.

On women and our
childhoods:

They try to wrap
Your spirit up
In neatly-boxed
Little packages.
The whole trouble is —
Whether the package
Is excellent enough.

I wept —
Coming over the sea
To Bombay, from Karachi.

There's the Bombay lighthouse.

At the Gateway to India

This is the bottom of the pit.

It is your determination
Which is the thing —
Not India or the Holy Land.

They came down into India
And got bloody-well lost —
There were no noble purposes.
Once here, when there was
No place else to go, they rose.

Yoga is yoga —
Yoga is for India
And sitting still
In this blessed heat.

Everyone is just
Lying around all day —
How wonderful.

You set tasks for
You to do
To keep yourself going.

Even the dogs are sleeping.

No one is going
To conquer this country,
No one could have — the heat.

See the warships
Lying still
Out in the harbor.

"The monsoon comes in" —
There is tremendous
Beauty in human life.

On friends:

People ally themselves
Against the forces of existence.
A man might just as well stand alone.

On artists:

You people are
All tricksters —
Using gimmicks.

Existence

It is just a problem to be unravelled like a knot.
The philosophers are blind and do not see these things any longer.
Knowledge is not science or discovery —
Knowledge is the Highest Way to live, the Highest Path to follow.
The problem is life, the choice is how to live.
The problems are money, housing, food, shelter, and honesty —
How to get what you desire without deception.
The problem is not whether I am or whether I am not,
The problem is not the *cogito,*
The problem is not how to bear it — the Stoic or the Taoist.
The problem is how to live the Highest Way.

There is only one way to go.
It is not to anywhere or anything,
But every day to toughen oneself
And face the tide.

Every effort is
A fight against
Non-existence.

My spirit is
Like a mite
Swimming around
In a deep, wide sea.

Now then,
Just keep
On going.

On the Indian boy's words:

Just to satisfy a man's penis,
Is that what marriage is for —
Just a license for fucking?
Can't he raise himself above that?

On thinking back to a time nineteen
years old:

Did he know then what joy there was
in the world?
Did he know what joy was waiting to
be unlocked
By the courage of his spirit
From the prison of his environment?

I was just beginning
To feel my own —
And every time
They'd call me home.

Bad eyes, fat belly, weak prick —
The prison sentences of
My environment.

Until I spit all that venom out,
There will be no relinquishment.

These all come from
A way of life
Which I deny.

Lord, I pray,
Help me to find a
Way out of the forest.

To the Israelis:

Don't go off the kibbutzim,
Don't develop a life
Which is too comfortable.
Don't become polluted
By modern conveniences.
Develop a life which
Is solely your own.
You have a second chance —
Don't throw it all away.

The danger is not from the Arabs
Though you may think it is.
The danger is from within
That you might sicken and die.
Love one another, cherish one another —
A light to the rest of the world.

I like living with the unknown.
Sight and planning are
The qualities of short-sighted men.

Coming into a port is like coming out
of blindness.
One does not know one will see ships
and sun and land
And lighthouses until one sees them.

This is the end of
The coming into
Bombay.

On Chowpatti Beach

Of course, it's easy to forget all here —
To practice yoga and bear it all.
No wonder the highest thing for them
Is to purge themselves of women.

The bottom of the world is fighting,
The basic emotion is fear,
The pride of the world is courage.

I live as long as it is possible to live.
All this running around after things
    and preparation is foolishness.

India is a cold world.
They do not help
Or love one another.

To love a country, to love a person —
Are these both lost to me?
Is there no other to love —
And yet I long to love.

There are countries —
You've created unconditional war
between us.
I'd rather fight and die with my
own people.

On hitchhiking to India:

Where was it leading to —
The Promised Land?
Therefore why should
You have bothered?

On thinking of a love's child by
another:

Lord let it die, but let her live.

If I could hold her in
My arms again I'd weep.
Yes, I tell you,
If I could hold her in
My arms again I'd weep —
The title of a poor song.

A long way home,
And to come to her,
I'd weep for the first time.

You know,
If I
Could hold
Her in
My arms
Again
I'd weep.

The white moon is coming out.

A hope that keeps
Coming in and out —
The moon that keeps
Coming in and out.

Hope

A hope that's going to carry
me
All the way around the world
again.

I'd
Throw away
A thousand things.

On yogis:

They give up trying
And then they learn
To live the other
way.

There's nothing to do
Except provide for oneself —
Shelter, food, sex.
All the rest are just amenities.

Turning the Corner

You set things up and, then,
Revolve around them
Like a pole.

A word in the center of the unknown,
A word swimming around in the sea,
A word in the blackness of the mind,
A word upon the lips,
A word in other people's ears —
A word which makes a future pathway known.

To a waiter I did not tip:

I swear, by God, this day
To treat every man the same
Regardless of his position.

Thoughts at the Beach Candy Swimming Club
— "For Whites Only" —

It's always the weakest part of the race
That creates a social bias against the others —
The upper-class in India,
The old-school-tie boy In England,
The pure-bred mediocritite in America —
One just comes into this world and goes out.

There it is — but you see
I don't mind sleeping outside,
So I have nothing to protect.

Women are very often immoral.
Be honest at all times with women
And you will, very often, get what you want.

To the honest harmless American:

It is not this that I hold against you,
But rather the covering over of your honesty
And, therefore, your deceit.
I've come to the other end of the world and
I know.

The great evils of society are
The laws people have made,
The "thou shalt"s and "thou shalt not"s —
No, it all depends upon the circumstances.
There is nothing worse than blind enslavement.

Essay on Slavery

Slavery is the adherence to a system.
Slavery weakens the individual.
There is only one freedom in this world,
That is, independence in mind as well as body.
The Lord is the only foundation —
Naked as you came into this world,
Naked you shall go out of it.

The only man who is capable of enjoying
All the pleasures of this world
Is the man who is not bound to it.
There is a new slavery in the world,
The slavery of men to goods,
The slavery of men to ideologies,
The slavery of man to systems beyond himself.
There should be only one slavery in the world —
The slavery of man to Justice.

No man is capable of enjoying all the happinesses
Of this world, though he say he be,
If he is blind, fettered, or in chains
Either physically, morally, or intellectually.
There are two kinds of beings in the world —
There are the enslaved and the free.
The heroes are the free;
The vast majority are the enslaved.
The men of courage, though poor-sighted,
Are struggling to achieve freedom.

The slavery of men to systems beyond each other:
Corporations, manners, style —
These unseen networks stemming
From the basest emotions of man —
This is the problem in the world today,
Not the slavery of men to each other.
The latter was simple and could be fought;
The former are far more complicated
And infect even the strongest of men,
Tying them in the end to their own basest
emotions.

It is a constant struggle — there is no end to it.
Your enemies are your closest friends,
The people you have grown up with,
Your parents, who are all worshipping it.
It is a subtle beast and waits to ensnare you
At any moment your guard is down.
Such is the world today and in such a world,
With men no longer in control, but unseen deities —
Secret mysteries in control of all,
There can be only destruction.

I tell you, if you rebel,
If you free yourselves,

Though you earn the enmity and spite
Of all those sickly creatures around you,
You in the end earn their respect
And undying love, for you are going
A long way towards freeing them.

The revolution cannot occur at the class level
Or at the national or even the international level.
It must occur at the personal level with every man
Throwing off his chains and becoming free —
With even the poor in spirit, the weak,
The infected, throwing away their crutches
And walking as free men and becoming free.

This sickness is impervious to class, to rich or poor.
It cuts across all monetary distinctions.
The rich are as enslaved as the poor, even more —
In this case, "blessed be the poor."
There is war in the world, a constant never-ending war,
No longer between nations, but between those who are slaves
And those who would be free.

It cuts across all borders and international boundaries,
It takes no heed of countries or political doctrines,
It takes no heed of class distinctions or of color or of race.
Its weapons are those of shame, poverty, and convention.
Its fruits are the fruits of all the ancient struggles —
Strength, power, women, and freedom from enslavement.
The battlefield is the college classroom,
The job section of the local newspaper —
The living room. It cuts across families.
It takes place at cocktail parties
And the spoils are another man's wife.

It is an age-old and perennial war
Between the conquered and the conqueror.
There is war in the world,
War between the weak and poor in spirit,
Between the short-sighted and the long-sighted,
Between the half-men and the slaves
And the perfect — the complete.

All things are at stake in this war,
All the age-old superhuman virtues:
Hospitality, honor, justice, pride.
It is a war between man's nature and himself,
Between the small in him and the big,
His power and his emotions,
The courageous and the weak,
The cringing and the strong,
The will to adventure and the will to convention.
On its outcome depends the fate of the world,
On its end, the end of the human tradition —
Not on the end of the world's politics and governments,
On its end, the bigness or smallness of man —
For man will either destroy himself,
In all the senses of that word, or go on.

Don't you see,
Why should you want to enslave me?
While we are fighting each other,
There is some higher force
At work enslaving us both.
You should help to free me.
We should work to free each other.

It is in my eyes
That the Lord sustains me —
As He sustained Moses
Coming down from Mt. Sinai.

See the empty street cars —
How ghostly they seem.

To understand
One's friends —
One's fellow men.

The only thing that blurs
One's vision in the end
Is lack of courage.

Here in these centers of men,
One studies man.
One walks around on
The groundlessness of his ways.
There, with the ants and the trees,
One walks as the others —
Thank God, there is also there.

In the city,
You've got to spend money.
Money is the language
Of the concentrations of men.
When you're out in the country,
Where the city ends, freedom begins.

When things get turned
In upon themselves,
They become sicknesses.

All desires are good.
It is only the world which perverts
and distorts them.
The thing to do is to learn to express them
With courage and honesty — and without distortion.

So there is it, Sri Ramikrishnan,
I don't want your Lord
To come to me.

I want the God of my fathers to come to me,
The God of Abraham, Isaac, and Jacob,
Because the people of this world
Are going to destroy each other.

These pleasures were put upon
This earth for you to enjoy,
The water was put upon
This earth for you to drink,
The food was put upon
This earth for you to eat —
But, just as too much food fattens
And too much water bloats — nothing
to excess.

You must go through it all.
If you cannot hold yourself up
Without denying, that is your fault.
If desires break your peace of mind,
That is your weakness — you must go through it.
If you deny, you are a coward —
Your evenness as brittle as your denial.

There is a union of pleasure in the
world.
We the young from every country
Vow to enjoy each other's bodies.

Poem on Dropping my Glasses into the Sea by the Gateway to India

The sun goes down, the bay,
The white and yellow houses,
The pink sky and a full moon
Just beginning to peep through,
The islands dotting the harbor,
The ships docked at their buoys,
The mooring bells ringing —
A boat sails out filled with people,
Sails leaning — a calm sea,
And everywhere there is peace.

Now, Lord, give me back my eyes.

A great weight has left my being.
I turn away from Jesus,
I turn away from beauty, light, and radiance —
To remain a Jew.

People need other people
To rally around.
Otherwise they become lost.

They don't know
Why they live,
Lord.

The Lord controls that too.
You must have lost your way.

It is the Lord God of Israel,
The Lord of Abraham, Isaac, and Jacob,
The Lord of Moses — strike down the idols!
The Lord of Law and the Lord of Justice —
Not the Lord of Peace.

O blessed darkness,
I'm going to go out
And celebrate tonight.
There's nothing wrong
with eating.

A holy moment.

Tomorrow I'm going to Delhi.

O you clever people, who have learned
To camouflage your desires for each other
Under thicker and thicker nets
Of rare spices, be honest!

They've tied me down
With stuttering
But, you see,
I've broken the chains.

The pull of this world is downpulling,
You must go out of society
To recreate yourself,
And then return to it,
Strong enough to exist through it.

This book is holy.

On Entente with Russia

The highest thing in the world
Is not the economic system.
The highest thing is Justice
And the means of bringing it about.
In the end the world will have to
Revolve about a system of laws,
Not about a system of production
Whether capitalism or communism.
The end is not the classless society —
This does not ensure a system of justice —
Or the dictatorship of the proletariat,
The end does not revolve about the U.N.
Or democracy or populism, or any one system.
The end revolves about bringing a system
Of Truth and Justice in the world
That will ensure the preservation
Of Peace and Justice for everyone —
And whoever gives it will be regarded
By the world as the great redeemer.

Not only is it within your power now,
But it is your duty as victors
In the Second World War,
Before the coming of Asia into prominence,
To bring this solution into the world
Before it is no longer within your power
Or possible — then no country will do it.
Then will only come destruction.

The fragmentation of the world continues
While you both stand impotently by,
Powerless and checkmated, as it were,
Because of each other to do anything about it.
Your present dilemmas — your past mistakes,
All result from adhering to an ideology
Or point-of-view too little for the present.

There is no longer any time for missteps.
The situation is in your hands now.
It is rapidly going out of your hands.
DeGaulle is your greatest friend
Because he shows you this in no uncertain terms.
Your true interests are with each other.
Time is your deathknell.
There can be no half measures or hesitation —
Either you take upon yourselves
The responsibility for the preservation
Of the world or default and watch helplessly
While the world destroys itself.

And this comes to you from a Jew —
Not the Jew of Israel, but the Jew of history:
"Thou shall love thy neighbor as thyself,"
"They shall beat their swords into ploughshares."
I am not a nationalist or a cosmopolitan.
I do not speak to you as an American.
I am interested in you solely as a means
Of bringing about this system
Of Peace and Justice into the world.
If you both fail, then I shall go to Israel.

To play a guitar, towards what end?
To make a living or to change the course of
history —
To be a bohemian, a wanderer, a stranger
Or to use the knowledge you have gained — not
for personal embellishment,
But to help bring about system of Truth and
Justice in the world?

On the Way to Delhi

The way in this world
Is like the path through the forest
With the forest continually disappearing.

It's wonderful to see
A fertile country again.

As soon as we stop the world
From running us around in
Little mechanical circles,
Then we become gurus (teachers).

I've been to India and, believe me,
The misery there is no worse than in any
suburban place.
Physical poverty is bearable.
Spiritual poverty is not — destruction.

The Arabs do not respect compromise,
The Arabs do not respect agreement,
The Arabs respect strength —
And who is the Lord God of Israel?
The Lord of Hosts, He is the Lord God
of Israel.

The justice? The justice is the Ten Commandments.
Do not give me this European, soft-soap nonsense.
The justice is an eye for an eye and a tooth for a tooth.
This was developed by your fathers who knew far more
than you.

In Delhi

I had to come to Delhi
And, from there,
He was going to show me
Which way to go — and lo,
He has.

Victory is sweet —
It is the sweetest thing.
Victory is the sweetest thing.

You people who spend
So much time asking,
Is He there or isn't He?
Follow your spirits and
See to where He leads
thee.

Beneeta

I think one of the reasons
I hold back from you is this —
I have never known pure beauty
before.
In America we know no such things,
Neither in hair or lips or form
So enslaved and adulterated have we
become.
I think one of the reasons
I hold back from you is this,
I have never known pure beauty
before.

The world goes through
A period of sinning —
And then old debts are
paid off.
Then they go on.

My father, my king,
I have sinned before Thee.
What I yearned for,
Such power — it was the Devil.

I'm going to bring back
The lost flock of Israel.

The knitting goes on.

I'm going to serve the Jewish
people.

I'm not an American,
Not an Israeli.
I'm Robert Eisenman.

Jewish history is completely
At odds with the rest of the world,
Even itself of the last two thousand years,
Except for the yearning to return home —
its destiny.
That is why you must not become confused
or forsake it for their gods.
That is why Israel is not the end.
There are ten million Jews in the world
And every one lost is a drop of blood lost —
Every one distilled, another one lost.

One Time Lost

She came to me then,
Thin and courageous,
One moment in Paris
I shall never forget.
If she were ever to come
To me again like that —
But no, lost, broken,
enslaved —
Forever submerged in
The eternity of time.

She came to me then
Thin and courageous.
If she were ever to
come
To me again like that,
I'd never let her go.

To an Olive Girl

I lost her.
I don't know how.
She stopped.
It could have been.
I grew forgetful —
Lost forever.

The struggle with the Arabs is
going to go on.
It is an epic struggle between
The whole of Jewish people
And the whole of the Arabs.
The Americans and Russians have
neutralized each other.

To the Americans
— In the style of Walt Whitman —

We have seen the end of science,
The end of man and his might —
I doff my hat at it.
It is but the hand of man,
The tool of man — I created it.
It does not exist without me.
I doff my hat at you,
You generations of science —
You generations of merchants.
I doff my hat and go on.

I lost my love through cowardice,
I lost my love through fear,
I lost my love through the breaches
Of a society that would but admit
enslavement.

I see the end —
The center is Jerusalem.

The Israeli army has got to whip
the Arab armies,
Israel must whip his brother Esau.
This is the prophecy —
Israel must put his unruly brother
Esau under control.

To go to Israel is to cripple oneself —
The Lord has not scattered us
To all parts of the earth
In order to cripple us.

I see a chance to tie up
The whole universe in
An aesthetic undertaking.

The Jewish people is
To be the tool of
This enterprise.

Do well, my brother.
Build mighty buildings —
One day we shall
Put them to some use.

I'm tired of the spectacle of this world.
Let me go down into the desert and lose
myself,
And let me come back a bronze lion with
the spirit of Judah.

Is the door then closed to me,
Has the Lord shut tight the bolt,
As He has the sight over my eyes?

When He will discomfitteth me,
He will discomfitteth me.

Debts obscureth sight.

Being broke is the utmost slavery.
There is only one freedom and
That is in making money.

O God, how I have lived,
For twenty-five years —
A slave.

If the cause is unjust,
Then you must always steel your nerve —
If the cause is just,
Then is there no steel necessary.

At Raj Gaat
(Gandhi's Tomb):

A memorial on earth to great men's
memories.

On Gandhi, Lincoln, and DeGaulle:

There is only one way to escape death —
That is, take every precaution
And then to boldly face it.

There is no peace here —
He used this method
To get something done.

I have gone through the eye of
the needle.

Then:

You chose to go back to America.
How could you choose to go back
To America without getting scarred?

This time
I'm going
To swim.

July 5th, 1962:

I shall use my brother one day
To rebuild the Lord's Temple
In Jerusalem.

Do not lose hope, dear father — do not lose faith.
You do not know what you have done,
But your tears have moved me very much.
You have sired two fine sons —
Both will swim in their own way.

Though I cannot see you,
I know you're there.
I feel you within me —
A sweet touch.
I feel your presence,
A perfumed cloud.

There is the end of something —
You cannot know the sweetness
At the end of something.
Until you get there,
All else is loved work —
The errors — the energy,
All become loved work.

It is not enough for
A man to be content
With his whole family.

I will not live like they.
Not when I have the chance
            to do it better.

There is only one woman I could love
And that woman came to me
For a moment in Paris, France.
I wonder if she knows herself —
The woman I loved — that moment of her?

You build your
Comfortable little houses —
You wall yourselves off from each other.

Compromise and non-violence is the
language of civilization.
Killing and Truth is the language of the
Old Testament.

The very unnaturalness
And inability of men
To perform these deeds is
The hypocrisy and immorality
Of the peoples of Europe
Where lip-service is paid
To an impossible religion —
Therefore all is condoned.

The Christians are
The little people
Who worship "Jesus" —
An extension of the
Lord.
What I look for is
The Highest in man.

Scholars are not
The true renderers,
For they care not
For the truth or evil
Of what they render.
The only true renderers
Are the new prophets.

Books, ideas, doctrines
Are a film before
The mind.

Sleeping outside in the
courtyard garden of the
Synagogue in New Delhi:

Lord,
If I am not to serve You,
Send Your serpent tonight.

I
Don't enjoy
Enjoying myself.

And so,
What have you
Got In the end?

To my brother:

Men are first of all men.
Professions make slaves of men.

My profession has to do
With other men's souls.

You have softened
The Lord's heart
Towards you.

The End of Passage to India

The step homeward will
Either be undertaken
Overland or by sea.

The Maccabees

What was it they struggled against then —
What is it that now infects you from Europe?
Who is it the Lord of Moses —
What was it you have forgotten
Clinging to your moneyed existences?

You can call me
"*Gur Arye*" now —
Son of the Lion.

I will come into contact with you
Ben Bella,
And your boast will be —
The cutting off of your head.

Everything is coming into view —
I've got the picture now.
There's not much more that I can do.

Everything is coming in handy,
All my former selves —
And my former past.

The bitter shrug of mortality.

He who seekest Israel shall
Neither tarry nor slumber.

On Japan:

If they have paradise
Then I don't want it.

My Lord, give us a new symbol.
Give us the sword of Eisenman.

The Lord has put me through
All this for some reason —
To show my People.

The light is burning
Very brightly
Tonight.

There is
Some force within me
Driving me on.

Knowing India as I know it now
Leads me to believe
Palestine is the center of the world
And not Europe or America, as I before
thought.

At every turn,
He recognizes the way
And chooses for me.

The blood is beginning
To stir up within me.
I feel it rising up from
The roots of the earth,
I feel it rising up from
The soles of my feet,
I feel it rising up from
The roots of this world.
It is time for me to bestir
myself.

I was born neither in life nor in death.
I was born in a soap bubble
Floating on a deep ocean —
I come alive now.

No I will not desert you
Israel,
Nor you my Jewish people.

One thing is certain.
I've laid the ground-
work well.

I don't think a man deserves
To enter a woman unless
He deserves her.

The ways of the Lord are infinite.

Up the Red Sea

To the Beats:

There is no longer any individual
destiny.
It is no longer possible
Not to be interested in politics —
Not to be interested in governments,
While you amuse yourselves
And bury your heads in the sand,
The world passes you by.

France helps no one,
Yet everyone loves France.

Off the Port of Alexandria, August 6, 1962:

Son of Man, prophesy against
the peoples,
Prophesy against the nations —
Tell them of their root in
blindness,
Tell them of their eyes deep
Within the pit of this world,
Tell them of their following all
the lesser ones
While the engines of destruction
Are unleashed overhead —
Tell them of their coming end.

The right hand of God is upon me,
The right hand of the Lord is on
my shoulder —
Call down the fiery whirlwind,
Call down the nuclear fireball.

Egypt of the rosy sunsets,
Egypt of the fires at night,
Egypt of the land rock rigid,
Egypt of the Sinai's might.

Red sky over Sinai,
Red mist upon blue hills,
Rocks crawling up into cragheads,
Fires burning on the Red Sea's shore.

AN AFTERWORD ON THE SIX-DAY WAR

April-June, 1967

Note to Reader

When Theodore Herzl, the founder of modern Zionism, after witnessing the Dreyfus Trial in 1894, wrote *Der Judenstaat* (*The Jewish State*) in 1895-6, outlining his program for a place of refuge and a homeland for the Jewish people; he speculated to himself that, if the idea was not realizable in actuality, it would at least make a good work of utopian or creative literature. The same might be said for the following pieces, written from April-June, 1967 in the midst of the emotional turmoil and spiritual and political crises leading up to and during the Six-Day War and reproduced here verbatim, just as they were transcribed then.

In order to appreciate them, the reader should consider the atmosphere of the time. It had been just over twenty years since the horrors of the Holocaust of World War II, wiping out as many as a third of all Jews in the world. Israel had been threatened by all the surrounding Arab Armies. In April of 1967, President Nasser of Egypt had closed the international waterway between Sinai and Saudi Arabia (known as the Straits of Tiran) to Israeli shipping, a *causis belli,* and in May the U.N. had spent days in futile debate, unable to do or agree on anything, before the then Secretary-General U Thant of Burma removed the U.N. Truce Supervisory Troops in Gaza, who were supposed to be enforcing the the terms of the Armistice signed in the aftermath of the 1948 War, making the outbreak of the Six-Day War inevitable.

A second Holocaust seemed certain just a quarter-century after the first. Israel seemed doomed to fall under the blows of the heavily Russian-equipped, surrounding Arab armies. All seemed lost, but from June 5th to June11th, 1967, as if by some miracle, the very opposite of what everyone expected transpired. These few pieces perhaps express something of the emotions felt by myself as a young man witnessing these events and unable to do anything about them except express himself in biblical metaphor — words which just seemed to pour out of me at the time.

April 14th, 1967 — The Tiran Crisis

I saw two children playing today
And one was making the other's
passage impossible —
Challenging him, confronting him,
Barring him, and then running after
him.

Is this not then the plight of the Jew
throughout the centuries —
Everyone running after him,
Challenging him, confronting him,
And then running after him again?

Words Written after the UN Security Council Debate
May 24th, 1967

And where shall we go? " To America," you say,
"To anywhere — we don't care where."
But we are done fleeing, we are done running away.

Because we were stubborn and would not give in — but
we shall not give in —
Because we would not be absorbed like all the rest, you
chased us all over the world.
You — you people began it and now, once again,
We are in your hands again, our fate at your disposal —
We the outraged people, we the people who have refused
to die;

But it has been at your disposal before — but we shall
not give in —
You in the form of the Roman Empire exiled us,
Sent us packing, expelled us from our land,
Ploughed under our religious shrines, made of Jerusalem
a waste place;
And, because we were stubborn, you chased us,
Because we would not give in — but we shall not give
in —
You tormented and tortured us and would not allow us to
live as part of your world;
And then you fed us into the gas chambers and deci-
mated our race —
But there were still some of us left who would not give in.

And then, when we wanted to go back to our own land,
You said, "No, you cannot go back. There is someone else
living there now."
But where shall we go — where would you have us go?
And so we said, "We shall go back — there is room for
us there";
But you made it difficult for us and so we fought,
Coming out of the concentration camps;
And then you left us to our own devices — in the
lurch, as it were,
To deal with the problems which you had created,
Though you had promised us and said you would
stand by us —
And so we had to fight again.

And now, once again, we are in your hands again —
Once more, we the outraged people, we the ever-recurrent
exiles,
We the ever-present refugees — we the people who have
refused to die,
Though you all wished us dead a thousand times,

Though your theology proclaims the fact that we
should live —
Once more, we are in your hands and your cross to
bear — to deal with as you see fit.
O Lord, lament that execrable day that, once more, we
should be in your hands
And at your mercy, for I have no confidence in your mercy.

But I tell you this, I swear it, that it be upon my heart —
As the Lord has "engraven" us upon the "palms" of His
"hands" —
If you let us down now, as you have every other time in
ours the most importune of pasts,
For your own individual, separate, and picayune motives,
I curse you — and my curse shall ring down the ages,
For none of you shall escape the fiery and horrendous fate
you reserve for us, not one of you —
And you shall all tread the path you have condemned us to
tread before you.

And hear my words — hear them, as you heard all my
brothers before me
In whom you have put so much faith, as you heard Moses'
(or Musa's) blessing and his curse,
For if you do this to us now, when we are only the Rem-
nant left,
I swear that not one of you shall escape a fiery and horrific
death
Worse than anything you have reserved for us.

And one final word before I'm done,
And hear it, hear it so that this time you know — this time,
let there be no mistake,
For this time we shall fight for we are "the Remnant,"
We shall fight to the last man as we did in the Warsaw

Ghetto
And at the time of Bar Kochba — as we did at the Fortress of Masada,
For it shall not be so easy to dispose of us now.
But I say these things mainly for your own souls rather than our own —
For the Holocaust, which you have inflicted and intend to inflict upon us,
Shall itself be inflicted upon you.

May 26th, 1967:

The forces of the world are roaring down the tracks like railroad trains.
There is no escaping them; they are tearing down their respective lines.
They are massing out of the East, the other side of the world —
And where do you stand America? You stand nowhere.

It is not a question of rights of passage or the Straits of Tiran or of this or that ploy.
The question is whether you are going to stop them
Or whether you are not going to stop them —
And they are all together in this — make no mistake about that
Or allow yourselves to be deceived; for, in time,
They will all be coming to eradicate your world —
To be sure, there is nothing so marvelous about your world,
Nothing that should cause one to wish to save it,

But the problems that exist in it are all internal and soluble,
If the proper attention were paid to them — which it is not;
But the problems they are bringing in their wake are insoluble
And will mean the end of Western civilization as you know it
And a return to the blood-chilling and barbaric cruelty of the past
Where all modern conveniences — all jet planes, ocean-going transport,
And new means of computation and communication —
Will simply be tools at their disposal (or yours),
Instruments behind which lies the face of man itself,
To use as they (or you) choose or see fit.

This is the problem in the world today
And this is the reason why all these forces are completely out of control —
And, in such a world, this is also why, America, in the end you will have to face them
Or be swept away like all the rest — your predecessors.

To America — May 26th, 1967:

And do you think you are in any different position than Israel?
Do you think that after they do away with Israel
They will not be in a position to do the same to you?
Don't you think that one day you will be in the same position as she?
Do you think that after they are done with her, they will

not, then, turn to you
And that you, too, will then be surrounded by the masses of
the peoples of the earth —
From Russia, China, the Arab world, Africa —
And don't you think one day they will cut off your oil,
Anyhow, when they see how easily it can be done?

And who do you think will come to rescue you then?
Do you not think that you, too, will then be alone —
And who will come to your aid and stand by your side?
Therefore, I say unto you, stand by her now and help her,
For she is but a miniature embodiment of you,
Alone in an uncharted and unfriendly sea —
If ever you wish to avoid the same circumstance yourself.

June 5th, 1967 — On the Israeli Invastion: The Outbreak of the War

Fight, you bastards, fight like Hell,
For we are avenging the wrong done us
Twenty centuries ago at the hands of the Romans —
For without that wrong, there would have been no such
thing as "Christianity,"
There would have been no "Islam" —
Nor would there ever have been such a thing as "the Arab
Empire."

Fight, you bastards, fight like Hell,
For we are making a new beginning —
We are doing the impossible and showing the world it can

be done —
Just twenty years after coming out of the concentration
camps,
And now, turning back the hands of time.

Fight, you bastards, fight like Hell,
For you are avenging your brothers and the defeat
They suffered at the hands of the Roman Empire —
A defeat that never should have been,
A defeat they suffered only because the other was too great;
And you are avenging the gas chambers —
The final effect of that defeat twenty centuries later.

Fight, you bastards, fight like Hell,
For we are sorry it has to be at the expense of our Arab
brethren,
But they are so pumped up with their own excitability,
Childishly indulged by the Western Powers into thinking
themselves indispensable —
So infatuated by the thought of their own importance,
the idea of their own magnificence,
Which never would have been except for our expulsion
And the total inability of the West to deal with the Middle
East.

Whoever heard of "*a world of harb*" and "*a world of Islam*" —
Whoever heard of land once conquered that could never be
relinquished?
This is not rational, this is not a religious imperative,
But a conceit, a pride — this is *hubris.*

So fight, my brothers, fight like Hell,
For Israel must put his wild brother Esau under control.
This is the prophecy —
"Israel must put her unruly brother under control."

To Orde Wingate — June 6th, 1967

Orde Wingate, this is your day —
It is you who foresaw what we could become,
It is you who foresaw the tremendous fighting strength
latent in a Jewish Army;
And it is you who wished to lead us before your life
was cut short.
But never fear, you are with us, you are leading us —
And perhaps it is better this way;
May God forgive me for having uttered those words —
Through the brave fighting men you prepared,
Through the men you trained, even at our Command.
Thank you, Orde Wingate, for we owe a great debt to
you.

THE NEW PASSOVER
HORSE AND RIDER HAS THE LORD OVERTHROWN IN THE DESERT — A NEW SONG OF MIRIAM
June 7th-11th, 1967

1

Horse and rider has the Lord overthrown in the desert,
Horse and rider has He overthrown in Sinai, leaving their
charred bodies to decompose in the burning sun.
Tank and tankman has the Lord thrown down in the desert —
twisted metal and rotting flesh,
Leaving the burned-out hulks, the torn treads, the shattered
turrets,
The scorched flesh of their combatants lying in the shifting
sands, the blistering sun,
Where first He delivered the Law unto Moses, His command-
ments to the rest of the world.

2

Horse and rider has the Lord overthrown in Sinai — tankman
and tankcrew,
And with His powerful right arm He has swept the rows of
their empty jet aircraft off their runways
As His screaming jets bore down out of the North and West
into the early morning sun
As they stared incredulously, shattering their hopes with rolling
pinpoint explosions,
Leaving the ruined metal tubes of their new jet aircraft in little
piles of twisted wreckage and oil slicks
Along the sides of runways in villages and cities around the
whole of the Arab world.

3

Horse and rider has the Lord thrown down in Sinai, tank and
tankman by the shores of the Red Sea,
Twisted Centurions and broken metal swept away in the roar of
blocked-up waters returning.
Corpses and rotting flesh has He left behind in the desert to
once more reaffirm His will to the rest of the world.

4

Call them from the East, call them from the West. I shall gather
them from the North.
To the South, I shall say, hold not back — it is the Lord of Hosts
who speaks.
I shall gather them up from all the corners of the earth and
return them to this land.
So stand aside all you nations of the earth, lest you get burned in
the burning,
For the Lord has commanded it — He has commanded the
gates of His Holy City, Jerusalem,
Be flung open before the faces of His homeless refugees and bid
them, enter.
Rebuild the ruined buildings, rebuild the waste places, make the

desert bloom.
The Lord has charged His people after an exile of two thousand years, after numerous tribulations and sufferings,
And endless trials and persecutions, to return and repossess the land, repossess the waste places,
Repossess the desert — the land He promised unto their ancestors, Abraham, Isaac, and Jacob, whom you all know.

5

So stand aside all you peoples of the earth, for horse and rider has the Lord thrown down in the desert,
Tankman and tankcrew, halftrack and armored personnel carrier.
The Lord has commanded it — as He did the waters of the Red Sea to part into two long waves.
See and be confounded, you peoples of the earth who claim to pray to His Holy Name
But, in reality, know only an offshoot of Him — a breath or scent of His loveliness.
Know the awesome majesty of the Lord God of Hosts, the Lord of Abraham, Isaac, and Jacob,
The Lord of the Psalms of David. See and be confounded, for the Lord of Hosts has commanded it,
And no man — not even the Russians — can stand before His mighty will.

6

Enough you Russians, however fertile this situation might seem to you,
For the Lord of Hosts is becoming angry and you too shall suffer the effects of His wrath
If you continue along the path of innuendo and falsehood you have already embraced,
For the Lord's fury will descend upon you as well. He demands your truthfulness now —
Truth shall be His signpost, not policy fabrications and equivocations, not disinformation,
For the Lord of Hosts is growing very angry and His wrath shall

be kindled against you too,
For He holds the sword of His vengeance poised above the entire length and breadth of your land.
So control yourselves, put a break upon your tongues, and heed the words of the ambassador of His people Israel,
For there is Truth flowing from that tongue — Truth the serum that will heal the world and set the peoples free.

7

For this is a new age, not an age of threats or counterthreats, violence or counter-violence,
Not an age of half-truths and lies, of propaganda violations and distortions,
Not an age of opium— any opium — so long as it soothes the misery of the masses, a dose of exhilaration and jubilation,
A taste to cure the pent-up frustrations of their shabby lives — a sip you often transform into frenzy.
But an age of the Lord God of Hosts and the cornerstone of that age shall be Truth —
Truth to distinguish between what really exists and what does not,
So there will be no inaccurate assessment of one's own capabilities.
For without that vital foundation upon which to base one's own judgements,
There can be only disillusionment and bitterness — a new age,
So even the downtrodden, the poor in spirit, will know their own capacities
And, even though advancement will come slowly, their hopes will not be shattered
And there will be no anger and frustration leading to frenzy and destruction —
But rather the progress of the world will go forward along its own independent path, slowly, sure-footedly, steadily.

8

So enough of this blustering, these false charges and counter-

charges which do nothing but inflame the world.
The time has come for you to cease. Beware the unrestrained flaunting of your own power —
You go too far and provoke the Lord of Hosts, for the cries of the oppressed and downtrodden have reached His ears.
Halt and cooperate, lest the violent anger of His wrath fall upon you a second time this century,
Striking down all that you have reconstructed, consuming all you hold precious,
And the end with which you threaten others shall itself be visited upon you, erasing all your generations from the earth.
The Lord's hand was in this. He has made good His promise unto Jacob,
He has made good His promise unto His people. Tank and tankman has He overthrown in the desert,
He has overthrown their horsemen — yea, all of them — and scattered their bones in the drifting sands
To be picked clean by vultures and bleached white in the midday sun.

9

Is this a victory song? Yes, it is a victory song — a celebration, a jubilation,
For the Lord has given victory unto Zion over all her enemies, as He promised so long ago.
So know, all you peoples of the earth, the awesome majesty of the Lord God of Hosts.
He has made good His promise unto Zion to redeem His people
And the Messianic Age of the Peoples of the Universe has begun.
Know it all you peoples and behold, for the Messianic Era has begun —
We proclaimed it at the beginning and we proclaim it at the end. The Lord has thrown down false prophets,
He has left the bones of their people rotting in the sun, leaving the shrieks of their insanity trail away into the desert.

10

Know you that the Lord is a great warrior. For a moment He let the fate of His people hang in the balance,
Suspended by the thickness of a single thread — and He could have cut that thread
With a single sweep of His powerful right arm if He wished to, but He preferred not to. He chose to do otherwise
And He did this as a lesson to you men, so you could see the awesome power He controls.
The Lord is magnanimous and great, the Lord is mighty and overwhelming. He preferred to usher in the Messianic Age
By the thickness of a single thread, the space of the eye of a needle — so know it all you peoples and give thanks.

11

And once more the Mountain of the Lord shall be established in the High Places,
The Temple of the Lord shall be established in Jerusalem and all nations shall come unto it,
For He has exonerated His people. He has purged them of their religious blight. The Lord has struck down false prophets.
He has stuck down His enemies and all the host that stood against Him from among the peoples of the world,
For the Lord abhors the language of compromise, the Lord abhors the prevaricators.
Israel among the nations has turned her back in prevarication and compromise.
Having paid the ultimate price for her indecisiveness, now she is following the path of absolute Righteousness.
Her example has astonished the nations, left their mouths dumbfounded, their eyes agape — silenced their tongues.

12

Know you, the Lord is a great and mighty warrior, know you He discomfits His enemies,
Know you, the Lord really is the Lord of Hosts — not the Lord

of all hosts, but all the Hosts of Righteousness —
So skip, my people, dance upon the streets, carry the news down to Eilat and deliver it up to Degania.
Let Ashkelon, Dan, and Hebron hear of it, and let it be brought up to Jerusalem.
Know you, the Lord is a mighty and great warrior — He discomfits His enemies
And leaves their bodies to rot in the desert, their bones bleaching in the burning sands,
To show there is no compromise when it comes to questions of Truth and Righteousness.

13

And so has He punished those of His people who prevaricated and held back and let not one escape unscathed.
So He has punished the slippery-tongued and squealing hearts of the Indians
And that compromising and vacillating tiny giant America.
He has punished the mischievous machinations of the naughty and always dangerous Russian bear,
The adventurism of their chess games and their total disregard for Truth
And the basic concepts of decency and fairplay — to love your neighbor as yourself and respect your enemy.
So has He punished the Arabs — Isaac's brother Ishmael and Israel's brother Esau — their wild frenzies,
Their romantic posturing and self-deception, their vainglorious distortions.
What is the rhythm at present of their soul, intoxicated by the sound of its own exhilaration,
Other than a riot of voices out of control — a voice that needs to be put under control?
The Lord has punished all His enemies and allowed His people Israel, as foretold long ago,
To return to their land — He has succoured His sheep.
He has also permitted the voice of prophecy, so long still, to return among them,
This time never to go forth or be extinguished again. The Lord

discomfits His enemies.

14

And hear you this, you nations of the earth, for we are singing a
battle song now, a celebration — a jubilation.
The armies of His enemies did the Lord throw down in the desert —
The armies of the Ishmaelites together with the Children of
Ham,
The armies of Pharaoh did He overthrow in the desert, leaving
not a single one escape alive to tell of it.
Their bones bleach the rocks and their blood runs into the
trackless wastes, coloring them red —
The Lord discomfits His enemies. Like men, the Lord abhors
the language of prevarication and compromise
And we are singing a battle song now, a celebration — a paean
to God.

15

And is it not strange that this thing should have taken place in
Sinai near Suez,
Where the Children of Egypt chased the Children of Israel so
many millennia ago?
Is it not strange that we have made up for that humiliation three
thousand five hundred years later
After embarking on that long, great wandering so many centuries ago?
And is it not strange that this defeat should have taken place at
the hands of the Children of Israel —
Those same former children who begged their masters to let
them go, but the Children of Pharaoh pursued them
Into the wilderness and would have taken them back into slavery were it not for the intervention of their Lord.
And now these same former Children of Israel with a mighty
hand have pursued the Children of Egypt
Into the wilderness of Sinai and slain them there, letting only a
few escape alive.

And is it not strange that the Children of Israel have avenged themselves on the Children of Ham
And their wild brother Esau in the same place they suffered that humiliation so many centuries ago?

16

The Lord is a mighty warrior, the Lord is a great charioteer. He has let our aircraft through their radar nets
Without as much as a single "blip" appearing on their radar screens.
And from where did all those missiles of destruction come, from where did those deadly wings emerge,
Wave after wave, to destroy the well-ordered rows of Egyptian jet aircraft before ever they took off?
The Lord is a flight of Mirages and Mysteres. He is a squadron of Fouga Meisters.
He has littered the desert with their burned-out trucks and half-tracks
And strewn the sands with their bodies, watering the earth with the libation of their blood.

17

And all the Egyptian homes which will be empty this night waiting for their loved ones to return,
For the Angel of Death did hover over all the houses of the Egyptians and claimed all their firstborn and finest,
But the houses of the Children of Israel did He pass over —
Know you the Lord is a mighty warrior, the Lord is a missile battery.
He is a squadron of Pattons and Centurions, a brigade of mechanized infantry, and steel has rolled over the Egyptians.
And see where He has done it, know where He has discomfitted them — in Sinai by the mouth of the Red Sea
Where He caused the backed-up waters to return and drown the chariots of the Egyptians, horse and man —
In Sinai near Suez, where the Children of Israel fled, at the Mitla Pass, not far from

Where the Lord first delivered His Commandments to Moses.
The Lord has thrown them down in Sinai
And scattered their bones in the desert, leaving almost every home in Egypt bereft of at least one man.

18

The Lord has prepared a table before me, He has prepared me a place to lie down upon and opened up the land before me.
Three weeks before my coming, He has flung open the gates of the Old City to greet me,
He has flung open the boundaries and the land is free again. O Lord, is this not an incomparable gift You have given me?
And how am I worthy of such a gift with all my cowardice and hesitation, how am I worthy —
And yet You have been bountiful and merciful, opening up the whole world before me.

19

And all nations shall come unto us in Jerusalem, all nations shall flow unto us in that site
And we shall build You a Temple there, the likes of which has never been seen before.
And we shall build it of marble and stone with a canopy a mile-square
And no one will have ever witnessed the equivalent thereof in the modern age of man,
But let us not be too vain, for we know how egocentric the works of man can appear to future generations.
But it is in Your honor and for Your glory that we build this thing —
You who have succoured us and overturned armies in our path,
You, who spread out our heritage before us and redeemed us, You who brought us back to Jerusalem,
Brought back the voice of prophecy with us, never more to be silent again. O Lord, we thank You for this wonderful gift,
We thank You for Your bountiful generosity and love — we thank You for this great thing.

20

I shall gather you up from the East and gather you up from the West and bring you home again,
From every corner of the world, to the land I promised unto your forefathers, Abraham, Isaac, and Jacob.
For behold, I promised My son Israel, "I have engraven you upon the palms of My hands" — you the people of My servant Israel,
You have kept the faith through every age, through disease, annihilation, and alienation,
Through wandering as despised outcasts throughout the earth for two thousand years.
I have inflicted upon you every scourge I could think of and you have asked no quarter, no compromise — only life,
As My servant Job before you — so return, hardened by two thousand years of history,
Hardened by your experiences and tempered in the fires of the furnaces of your destruction,
Return! Occupy the land which I the Lord have promised you as your inheritance.

21

Fling open the gates, O Jerusalem. Spread the tidings of gladness and great joy from city to city around the world,
For the Lord has succoured His people. He has commanded His Holy People to return —
Return and take over the cities, take over the waste places, take over the vineyards.
Occupy Jericho, Beth-El and Tulkarim, occupy Samaria, Shiloh, and Jerusalem.
Throw open the gates, O My people. Blast it upon your trumpets.Occupy Nablus and Shechem.
Occupy Bethlehem, Beit Jalla, and Beit Iksa, occupy Ramallah and Jenin.
Rebuild the waste places, O My people, rebuild the high places, replant the vineyards,
Roll away the rocks from the barren hillsides and make of the

land a garden — and plant,
For it will respond to your touch and bear fruit. It will send up shoots and vines in their seasons,
For truly I have given it unto you and your seed as an inheritance forever.

22

And I call upon the religions of the world — your offshoots — to stand aside, stand back,
Lest the fury of the Lord descend upon them, as it descended upon their ancestors those many ages ago,
Searing their idols, overturning their totems and sacred groves, for I the Lord have proclaimed it and given it.
I have said to My people, the Children of Abraham, Isaac, and Jacob, the Children of Israel, "You have suffered enough.
After two thousand years and annealed in the fires of affliction,
Return, for I have given this land unto you and your seed as an eternal monument to My greatness forever,
And never again, as long as the peoples of the earth shall live, will you be asked to go hence from or relinquish it."

23

And I have said unto the other nations of the earth, "Relent, lest a terrible burning overtake you as well.
Retreat from your stiffneckedness and self-importance, lest the anger of the Lord fall upon you,
Making you the holocaust you have attempted to make or have made others.
Fling open the gates of Jerusalem and spread tidings of great joy from city to city around the world,
For I have given this land as a first-fruit to the people of Israel, My firstborn,
And all of you know this, for you pray about it in your churches, mosques, and tabernacles every day."

24

And I say unto one of your shepherds in Rome, "Be humble
and be not arrogant. Read the Scriptures,
Which you claim to follow by tasting My 'body and blood' in
your services round the world every day,
For you are not the hand of God on earth — though ye claim
to be — but merely one of His many appendages.
So believe in My prophecies and be meek. Be flexible lest the
fate of the Roman Empire, whose extension you are,
Fall upon you as well. Lest your very sanctuary in Rome be re-
duced to cinder and ash,
And give unbegrudgingly to My people, the Jews, whom you
know and have persecuted for so long
And return My Holy City, Jerusalem, to them whose inheri-
tance it rightfully is."

25

And I say unto you Arabs, the Sons of Ishmael, Esau, and Ham,
"Be calm. Let your tempestuousness subside,
Lest you too be effaced from off the earth. For you are only the
servants of your brother Israel and your half-brother Isaac.
To them has gone the blessing and to you all the rest. And lest
you wish more of the curse
Than you have already drunk so deeply of these many centuries,
be generous to and magnanimous towards them,
Be gentle and protect them as, indeed, being older and stronger
by far you should,
For I have given the land unto them as an eternal resting place
for My glory forever.
To them, I have given the stones, the hills, and the religious
places — and to you, all the rest,
All the seas of the desert, under which lie such vast pools of oil,
and the other lands,
And all the wealth. For Ishmael shall indeed be a great nation
and the father of many princes,
But you must put aside your anger, your pride, your venom at
these your younger brothers

Who have been chastened in the fires of affliction and annealed
in the furnaces of destruction,
Work with them, cooperate with them, for only through their
hand and their blessing
Will I allow your land to blossom, your wilderness to bloom,
your wastelands to regain their fertility.
They are your charge and your legacy to protect but only
through their inheritance will you be blessed —
Indeed, you shall once again become a mighty people, but only
through their blessing will yours be fertilized.
So cherish them, keep them, turn the anger in your hearts away
from them and put it to more constructive use."

26

And you too, you peoples of the earth, "Prepare yourselves for
the wonderful Day of the Lord,
Foretold in the books of the Prophets, perverted and turned
away from, held back from and postponed, has finally arrived.
Prepare yourselves, all nations and peoples of the world, to come
up to the Temple of the Lord, My Sanctuary in Jerusalem,
Kept and guarded by My people Israel who shall once more
become a holy people, a people of priests.
Come up to Jerusalem for the Messianic Age of the Peoples of the
Universe has at last begun.
By the thickness of a single thread, by the wideness of the eye of
the needle — a new eternity,
A new era, a new age of man has been ushered in and all peo-
ples shall benefit from it.

27

So come in great planeloads and shiploads, and climb up the
Holy Mountain to the High Hill of the Lord in Jerusalem
Where, as a sign of My future uninterrupted presence there I
have established My people Israel.
For I have gathered them up from all the corners of the earth

and said to My holy seed, 'Return.
Return from the East, return from the West, return from the
South. To the North I have said, hold not back —
I have taken My seed up from Asia, Africa, Europe, and America,
first by ones, twos, and threes,
Then in busloads and shiploads, and finally as one great torrent
and flood,
That remnant promised so long ago in Ezekiel — the one-third
who were to survive.'
So come up all you peoples of the earth to the Mountain of the
Lord in Jerusalem and to His Holy Temple,
For I have chased the Syrians all the way back to Damascus and
there is no longer any doubt
That the Messianic Era has begun" — it is the Lord of Hosts
who speaks.

28

The Lord reached out with a strong right arm in the early
morning light and removed all their aircraft
From their runways right before their still sleep-filled eyes.
With one sweep of His powerful right arm, He has confounded
them
And wiped their empty new airplanes off their runways in cities
and towns
Around the whole of the Arab world, leaving them bewildered
and helpless, dazzled and bereft.
Know you the terrible anger of the Lord God and feel his po-
werful concussions,
The rolling pinpoint explosions of His strong right arm — and
behind them He has sent His armor over the desert
And caught them in their stupor, annihilating them, tanks, half-
tracks, jeeps, and vans — taxis, buses, and men,
The soldiers of the Army of the Lord of Hosts have poured
across the desert
And delivered the final blow of His overwhelming might.

While with His left hand, He removed the ramparts of the Holy
City of Jerusalem
And the soldiers of the Lord God of Hosts have stormed the
crumbling walls of the ancient Temple.
And He has flung open the gates of His Holy City to His people and bid them, once again, "Enter."

29

After two thousand years of suffering and endless wandering,
with a single sweep of His powerful right arm,
The Lord removed all the airforces of their enemies from before
His people.
In successive waves of attack, like winged cherubim out of the
past — Mirages, Fougas, and Mysteres,
In the space of three hours at twenty-five different airbases
around the whole of the Arab World —
At Cairo, Alexandria, Amman, and Jerusalem, Damascus, Suez, El
Arish, and Aswan; at Homs, Aleppo, Mosul, and Baghdad,
The Lord confounded them and left them helpless, breaking
their machines of war before their very eyes,
Flinging them down like so many matchsticks in twisted piles of
metal along the sides of runways,
Sweeping the unused rows of empty jet aircraft aside, leaving
nothing but little oil pools and mounds of twisted tubing.

30

The Lord with one sweep of His powerful right hand has left
them helpless and agape —
As the Angel of Death passed over all the houses of the Israelites
in the night
Leaving their firstborn alive and happy, only striking the firstborn of the Children of the Egyptians,
The Lord wiped away their armor and their airshields, and they
who would have abolished Israel, annihilating her people,

Leaving her towns empty and as wasteplaces, have themselves been ruined and left defenceless,
Their armies lost in the drifting sands and stones of the desert forever.

31

So let this be a lesson to all who hate Israel and presume to raise their voices
Against the Lord's Holy People, attempting to strike down her armies —
As the Lord lifted His right arm and stretched it over the Red Sea, parting the waters
To allow the Children of Israel to pass through dry-shod, then bringing the water back again
To overwhelm the charioteers of Pharaoh, drowning them in a watery grave;
So too in the early morning light, as they stared incredulously, did He remove the rows
Of their empty new jet aircraft right in front of their still sleep-filled eyes,
Piling them up in little heaps of twisted metal and oil slicks
Along the sides of runways around the whole of the Arab World.
So let this be a lesson to all who would pursue and persecute the Children of Israel,
Lifting up their voices against His almighty will and planting themselves stiff-necked against His inexorable desire,
For He has chased the Syrians all the way back to Damascus
And there is no longer any doubt that the most marvelous Era has begun.

32

Horse and horseman has He thrown down in the desert, tank-man and tankcrew alone in the desert
Where He caused them to be overthrown. See them there,

straggling in search of water,
Desperate bands stretched out across Sinai, strung out over the
deserted waste in long lines,
Their mouths parched, their wounds gangrenous, their feet shredded and torn,
Because they dared stand in the face of the will of the Lord of
Hosts,
Steeped in arrogance, their minds clouded by delusion and ignorance, groping towards any shrieking chimera —
In the poverty and misery of their daily existence, to relieve the
pent-up anger of their shallow lives,
Any overweening presumption — in their blindness and bewilderment they dared stand in the face of the Lord God of Hosts.
In the bottomless pit of their egos, fed by spite, disillusionment,
frustration, and terror
To grasp the few sweet straws of existence proffered to them as an
enticement by their rulers, they dared stand in the face
Of the Lord God of Hosts — so has He overthrown them as He
shall all the enemies of His Divine will.

33

The Lord is a mighty and great warrior. Armies and tank corps,
Jet fighter bombers and radar nets does He overthrow in His
fury.
The Lord's anger is very swift — it is like a white-hot fire on a
blistering heat-filled day.
The Lord's burning rage seared them into dumbness, their limbs
into blackness.
In His rage He has consumed them, in His rage He caused His
fire to fall upon them,
In His rage He has left them blind and forlorn, stumbling over
the sand,
In His rage has He overthrown them— the armies of Egypt.
He has overthrown Pharaoh and his mighty hordes in the
wilderness of Sinai

And left only a remnant of them, alone and tottering in the desert, dying of thirst and seven-days' sun-glare.
The Lord has thrown them down in Syria too and chased their broken armies —
The sons of Aram and Hazael — all the way back to Damascus.
He has sent the sons of Edom and the Moabites back over the Jordan to Amman
And left the armies of the Israelites standing alone and sentinel along its banks.
He has overthrown their bridgeheads, so that none may return
And, once more, broken through the walls of Jericho, scattering its inhabitants.
The Lord is a brigade of mechanized infantry, a mighty armored column, a squadron of Fouga Meisters.
The Lord is a Katyusha rocket battery — horse and horseman has He overthrown in the desert,
Tank and tankman, tankcrew and tank column, to once more reaffirm His will to the rest of the world.

34

The Lord is a mighty vengeance-taker full of rage — He has left them alone in the desert.
Their shoes have they cast aside. See them there, their starved remnants staggering with parched-dry mouths,
Tired and bruised with bleeding feet, to roam the rocks and sand of Sinai until they die of hallucination and thirst
Or are driven into insanity by the searing heat of His white-hot anger.
The Lord is a mighty warrior, horseman and charioteer has He overthrown in the desert,
Leaving them toothless and agape, dazzled and astonished at burning fire of His blistering wrath.

35

They are straggling in the desert, their flesh is burned and their
mouths are parched,
They are alone and lost without water, wandering the endless
mountain passes and rocks —
Away from the road where they drop from starvation, exhaustion, and seven-days' thirst.
Their bodies are lost and their bones, picked clean by vultures
and worms, are bleaching in the sun forever
Where first He delivered His Law in Sinai, His Commandments
to the rest of the world —
Because they have made Him, the Lord, very angry.

New York, June 7th-11th, 1967